The Modern Book

Baby Names

The Modern Book of
Baby Names

Hilary Spence

foulsham

LONDON • NEW YORK • TORONTO • SYDNEY

foulsham

The Publishing House, Bennetts Close,
Cippenham, Slough, Berkshire, SL1 5AP

ISBN 978-0-572-02585-4

Cover photograph by kind permission of Mothercare.

Design and illustration by Sarah Wilkinson

Printed in Great Britain by J. H. Haynes & Co. Ltd., Sparkford

Choosing your baby's name

Choosing a name for your new baby is a big decision. Only a very small number of people ever change their given names – and those usually for very specific reasons most often associated with show business! – so you are choosing a name which your child will carry with them throughout their lives, and which will come to define them as an individual. Daunting? Yes! Exciting? Certainly! And with this book you will have all the help you need to make the right choice.

You'll want to consider every aspect of the name you choose, making sure the first name goes well with the surname, the initials don't create an unfortunate combination and the name has the positive associations which match what you want for your child. Think about whether you like the popular forms of the name and whether you want to choose a name which your child will share with others, or which will make them stand out from the crowd.

Clearly organised in two main sections for girls and boys, this book offers you a broad selection of over 4000 traditional and modern names in an easy-to-browse format so that you can take your time considering the names you want to give your child.

To make your selection easier, go through the book and highlight your favourites, so that you can carry on thinking about your decision and reducing your short-list until you make that final and all-important choice.

Names tend to have cycles of popularity and the following list, published by the Office for National Statistics, shows the top 50 most popular names in England and Wales in 2006.

The increasing creativity and informality in naming children continues, so the lists often include shortened forms of traditional names in higher positions than the original names from which they are derived. Lucy is number eight, for example, but Lucille is not in the list. New entries in the girls' top-50 chart this year include Imogen, up 17 places, Sophia, up 13 places, and the return of an old favourite, Anna, up two places to number 50. Ruby is a high-riser, up 11 places, as is Jasmine, moving up 10 places to 31.

There is also a strong indication that celebrity plays a big part in parents' choices. Perhaps it's thanks to X-Factor winner, Shayne Ward, that Shayne's popularity as a name increased by 827 per cent over the past year, while Big Brother's Preston has seen his name move up 767 places – although neither quite make it into the top 50. New entries in the boys' top 50 include Muhammad, up 12 places, Lucas and Rhys, both up 10 places this year.

Muhammad is also one of the names that features twice: Muhammad at 44 and Mohammed at 22. Others are James at 6 with Jamie at 32; Sophie at 6 with Sophia at 49; and Isabella at 19 with Isabelle at 29 and Isabel at 44.

Boys: Top 50 Names

1	Jack	26	Adam
2	Thomas	27	Tyler
3	Joshua	28	Harvey
4	Oliver	29	Max
5	Harry	30	Cameron
6	James	31	Liam
7	William	32	Jamie
8	Samuel	33	Leo
9	Daniel	34	Owen
10	Charlie	35	Connor
11	Benjamin	36	Harrison
12	Joseph	37	Nathan
13	Callum	38	Ben
14	George	39	Henry
15	Jake	40	Archie
16	Alfie	41	Edward
17	Luke	42	Michael
18	Matthew	43	Aaron
19	Ethan	44	Muhammad
20	Lewis	45	Kyle
21	Jacob	46	Noah
22	Mohammed	47	Oscar
23	Dylan	48	Lucas
24	Alexander	49	Rhys
25	Ryan	50	Bradley

Girls: Top 50 Names

1	Olivia	26	Holly
2	Grace	27	Emma
3	Jessica	28	Erin
4	Ruby	29	Isabelle
5	Emily	30	Poppy
6	Sophie	31	Jasmine
7	Chloe	32	Leah
8	Lucy	33	Keira
9	Lily	34	Phoebe
10	Ellie	35	Caitlin
11	Ella	36	Rebecca
12	Charlotte	37	Georgia
13	Katie	38	Lauren
14	Mia	39	Madison
15	Hannah	40	Amber
16	Amelia	41	Elizabeth
17	Megan	42	Eleanor
18	Amy	43	Bethany
19	Isabella	44	Isabel
20	Millie	45	Paige
21	Evie	46	Scarlett
22	Abigail	47	Alice
23	Freya	48	Imogen
24	Molly	49	Sophia
25	Daisy	50	Anna

Girls

Abeer Arabic 'Fragrance'.

Abia Arabic 'Great'.

Abigail Hebrew 'A father's joy'.
Abagael, Abbe, Abbey, Abbie, Abby, Abigael, Gael, Gail, Gale, Gayla, Gayle, Gayleen, Gaylene

Abijah Hebrew 'God is my father'.
Abisha

Abnaki Native American 'Land of the morning'.

Abra Hebrew 'Mother of multitudes'.

Abrona Latin 'Goddess of beginning journeys'.

Acacia Greek 'Innocent'.

Acantha Greek 'Thorny'.

Accalia Latin Foster mother of Romulus and Remus, founders of Rome.

Achala Sanskrit 'Constant'.

Acima Hebrew 'The Lord's judgement'.

Acola Teutonic 'Cool.'

Actia Greek 'Ray of sunlight'.

Ada Teutonic 'Prosperous and joyful'.
Adda, Addia, Aida

Adabelle Latin 'Joyous, happy and beautiful'.
Adabel, Adabela, Adabella

Adah Hebrew 'The crown's adornment'.

Adalia Teutonic An early Saxon tribal name.

Adamina Latin 'From the red earth, mortal'. Also feminine of Adam.
Addie, Addy, Mina

Adar Hebrew 'Fire'.

Adara Greek 'Beauty'.

Adicia Greek 'Unjust'.

Addula Teutonic 'Noble cheer'.

Adelaide Teutonic 'Noble and kind'.
Adaline, Addi, Adela, Adelaida, Adele, Adelia, Adelina, Adelind, Adeline, Adelle, Dela, Della, Edelina, Edeline

Adelicia Teutonic 'Noble happiness'.

Adelinda French 'Noble and sweet'.

Adelphia Greek 'Sisterly'.
Adelfia, Adelpha

Adena Greek Accepted'.

Aderyn Welsh 'Bird'.

Adiba Arabic 'Cultured'.

Adiel Hebrew 'Ornament of the Lord'.

Adila Arabic 'Equal, like'.

Adima Teutonic 'Noble, famous'.

Adina Hebrew 'Voluptuous'. One of mature charm.

Adione Latin Goddess of travellers.

Adnette French from Old German 'Noble'.

Adolpha Teutonic 'The noble she-wolf'.

Adoncia Spanish 'Sweet'.

Adonia Greek 'Beautiful goddess of the resurrection'.

Adora Latin 'Adored and beloved'.

Adraima Arabic/Hebrew 'Fruitful'.

Adrienne Latin 'Dark lady from the sea'. Feminine of Adrian.
Adria, Adriana, Adriane, Adrianna, Adrianne, Hadria

Aelwen Welsh 'Beautiful brow'.

Aena Hebrew 'Worthy of praise'.

Aerona Welsh 'Like a berry'.

Aeronwen Welsh 'Fair berry'.

Afra Teutonic/Hebrew 'Peaceful leader' (Teutonic) or
'dust' (Hebrew).

Africa Celtic 'Pleasant'.
Affrica, Africah, Afrika, Afrikah

Agatha Greek 'Of impeccable virtue'.
Agace, Agata, Agathe, Agathy, Aggie, Aggy, Agueda

Aglaia Greek 'Splendour'.

Agnella Greek 'Pure'.

Agrippa Latin 'Born feet first'.
Agrippina

Ahuda Hebrew 'Praise' or 'sympathetic'.

Aidan Gaelic 'Little fire'. A girl with bright red hair.

Aiko Japanese 'Little love, beloved'.

Aileen Greek/Irish 'Light' (Greek) or an Irish form of Helen.
Aila, Ailee, Ailey, Aili, Aleen, Alene, Eileen, Elene, Ileana, Ilene, Iline, Illeana, Illene, Illona, Ilona, Isleen

Ailsa Old German 'Girl of cheer'.
Aillsa, Ailssa, Ilsa

Aimee Popular variation of Amy.

Ainsley Gaelic 'From one's own meadow'.
Ainslee, Ainslie

Aisha African/Arabic 'Life'.
Ashia

Aisleen Gaelic 'The vision'.

Aisling Old Irish 'Dream' or 'vision'.

Akasuki Japanese 'Bright helper'.

Akili Tanzanian 'Wisdom'.
Akela, Akeyla, Akeylah

Alame Spanish 'Stately poplar tree'.

Alana Celtic 'Bright, fair one'.
Alain, Alaine, Alanah, Alanna, Alayne, Alina, Allene, Allyn, Lana, Lanetta, Lanette

Alarice Teutonic 'Ruler of all'. Feminine of Alaric.
Alarica, Alarise

Alba Latin 'White'.

Albina Latin 'White lady'.
Albinia, Alvina, Aubina, Aubine

Alcina Greek 'Strong-minded one'.
Alciana, Alcinette

Aldara Greek 'Winged gift'.

Aldis Old English 'From old house'.

Aldora Anglo-Saxon 'Of noble rank'.
Aelda, Aeldra

Alegria Spanish 'Happiness'.

Alena Russian Form of Helen.
Aleen, Aleena, Alenah, Alene, Alenka, Allene, Alyna

Aleria Latin 'Eagle-like'.

Aletta Latin 'Little wing, bird-like'.

Alexandra Greek 'The helper of mankind'. Feminine of Alexander.
Alejandra, Alessandra, Alex, Alexa, Alexandrina, Alexia, Alexina, Alexine, Alexis, Alix, Lexie, Lexine, Sandy, Sandra, Sasha, Sashenka, Zandra

Alice Greek 'Truth'.
Alecia, Aleece, Alesha, Aletha, Alethea, Alicea, Alicia, Alika, Alisa, Aliss, Alissa, Alithia, Alla, Allie, Allis, Ally, Allyce, Allys, Alyce, Alys, Alysia, Alyssa, Elisa, Elissa, Elke

Alida Latin 'Little winged one'.
Aleda, Aleta, Alita, Leda, Lissie, Lita

Alima Arabic 'Learned in music and dancing'.

Alisha Greek/Sanskrit 'Truthful' (Greek) or 'protected by God' (Sanskrit).
Aleesha, Alesha

Alison Teutonic/Greek 'Truthful warrior maid' (Teutonic) or
'alyssum flower' (Greek).
Allie, Allison, Allyson

Aliya Hebrew/Arabic 'Sublime, exalted'.
Aliyah

Allegra Latin 'Cheerful'. As blithe as a bird.

Alma Latin 'Cherishing spirit'.

Almeda Latin 'Ambitious'.
Almeta

Almira Arabic 'Truth without question' or 'Princess'.
Almeira, Almeria, Elmira

Alodie Anglo-Saxon 'Wealthy, prosperous'.
Alodia

Aloha Hawaiian 'Greetings'.

Aloisa Teutonic 'Feminine'.
Aloysia

Alphonsine *Teutonic* 'Noble and eager for battle'.
Alfonsine, Alonza, Alphonica, Alphonsina

Alta Latin 'Tall in spirit'.

Althea Greek 'The healer'.
Aletha, Alethea, Althee, Altheta, Thea

Altheda Greek 'Flower-like'.

Aludra Greek 'Virgin'.

Alula Latin/Arabic 'Winged one' (Latin) or 'the first' (Arabic).
Alloula, Allula, Aloula

Aluma Hebrew 'Girl'.

Alura   Anglo-Saxon 'Divine counsellor'.

Alvina   Teutonic 'Beloved and noble friend'.
Alvine, Alvinia, Vina

Alviona   Teutonic 'Beloved and noble friend'.
Alvine, Vina

Alvira   Teutonic 'Elfin arrow'.

Alvita   Latin 'Vivacious'.

Alysia   Greek 'Unbroken chain'.

Alyssa   Greek 'Sane one'. White flower.

Alzena   Arabic 'Woman'. The embodiment of feminine charm and virtue.

Amabel   Latin 'Sweet, lovable one'.
Amabella, Amabelle

Amadea   Latin 'The beloved of God'.

Amadore   Italian 'Gift of love'.
Amadora

Amala   Arabic 'Hope'.
Amla

Amana   Hebrew 'Faithful'.

Amanda   Latin 'Worthy of being loved'.
Manda, Mandie, Mandy

Amanta   Latin 'Loving one'.

Amany   Arabic 'Aspiration'.

Amapola   Arabic 'Flower'.

Amara   Greek 'Of eternal beauty'.
Amargo

Amarantha Greek 'Unfading'.

Amaris Latin/Hebrew 'Child of the moon' (Latin) or 'promised by God' (Hebrew).

Amata Latin 'Beloved'.

Amber Arabic/Sansrkit 'Jewel' (Arabic) or 'the sky' (Sanskrit).
Amberly, Ambur

Ambrin Arabic 'Fragrant'.

Ambrosine Greek 'Divine, immortal one'. Feminine of Ambrose.
Ambrosia, Ambrosina

Ameerah Arabic 'Princess'.

Amelia Teutonic 'Industrious and hard working'.
Amalee, Amalia, Amalie, Amealia, Amelea, Amelie, Ameline, Amelita, Mell, Mellie, Milicia, Mill, Millie

Amelinda Spanish 'Beloved and pretty'.
Amalinda, Amelinde

Amena Celtic 'Honest'. One of incorruptible truth.
Aminaz

Amethyst Greek Semi-precious stone.

Amilia Latin 'Affable'.

Amine Arabic 'Faithful'.
Amina

Aminta Greek 'Protector'.
Amintha, Aminthe

Amira Arabic 'Princess, cultivated'.

Amity Old French 'Friendship'.

Amorette   Latin 'Darling'.
Amarette, Amoret, Amorita, Morette

Amrit   Sanskrit 'Ambrosia'.

Amy   French 'Beloved friend'.
Aimee, Am-ee, Ami, Amie

Anala   Sanskrit 'Fiery'.

Anamari   Basque Derivation of Anna Maria.

Anastasia   Greek 'She who will rise again'.
Ana, Anstice, Stacey, Stacia, Stacie, Stacy

Anatola   Greek 'Woman of the east', 'sunrise'. Feminine of Anatole.
Anatholia, Anatolia

Ancelin   Latin 'Fairest handmaid'.
Celine

Anchoret   Welsh 'Much loved'.

Ancita   Hebrew 'Grace'.

Andeana   Spanish 'Traveller on foot'.

Andrea   Latin 'Womanly'. The epitome of feminine charm and beauty.
Aindrea, Andre, Andreana, Andree, Andria, Andriana

Andromeda   Greek 'Ruler of men'.

Aneira   Welsh 'Honourable' or 'golden'.

Anemone   Greek 'Windflower'.

Angela   Greek 'Heavenly messenger'.
Angel, Angelina, Angeline, Angelita, Angie

Angelica   Latin 'Angelic one'.
Angelique

Angharad   Welsh 'Free from shame'.

Angwen Welsh 'Very beautiful'.

Aniela Italian 'Angel'.

Anika Czech 'Gracious'. A form of Anne.
Anneka, Annika

Anila Sanskrit 'Wind'.

Anna Popular variation of Anne.

Annabelle Combination Anne/Belle.
Anabel, Annabel, Annabella, Annie, Bella, Belle

Anne Hebrew 'Full of Grace'. One of the most popular feminine names in the UK and the name of a British queen and several queens consort.
Ana, Anita, Anitra, Ann, Anna, Annie, Nan, Nana, Nancy, Nanetta, Nanette, Nanice, Nanine, Nanna, Nanon, Nina, Ninette, Ninon, Nita

Annette French 'Grace'. A familiar form of Anne.
Annetta

Annissa Arabic 'Charming, gracious'.

Annona Latin 'Fruitful' or 'annual crops'. The Roman goddess of crops.
Annora, Anona, Nona, Nonnie

Anselma Norse 'Divinely protected'.
Anselme, Selma, Zelma

Anthea Greek 'Flower-like'. One of delicate, fragile beauty.
Anthia, Bluma, Thea, Thia

Anthelia Greek 'Facing the sun'.

Antonia Latin 'Beyond price, excellent'. Feminine of Anthony.
Anthonia, Antoinette, Antoinietta, Antoni, Antonina, Netta, Nettie, Netty, Toinette, Toni, Tonia

Anusha   Hindi 'A star'.

Anwyl   Welsh 'Precious'.

Anya   Hebrew 'Grace, mercy'.
Ania, Annia

Anysia   Greek 'Whole'.

Anzonetta   Teutonic 'Little holy one'.

Aphra   Hebrew 'Female deer'.
Afra

Appoline   Greek 'Sun'.
Apollene

April   Greek 'The beginning of spring'.

Aquilina   Latin 'Little eagle'.

Arabella   Latin 'Beautiful altar'.
Arabela, Arabelle, Aralia, Arbel, Arbele, Arbelia, Arbelle, Bel, Bella, Belle

Aradhana   Sanskrit 'Worship'.

Aramanta   Hebrew 'Elegant lady'.
Aramenta

Araminta   Greek 'Beautiful, sweet-smelling flower'.

Ardana   Sanskrit 'Restless one'.

Ardath   Hebrew 'Field of flowers'.
Ardatha, Aridatha

Ardelle   Latin 'Enthusiasm, warmth'.
Arda, Arden, Ardelis, Ardella, Ardere

Ardra   Latin 'Ardent'.

Ardun   Welsh 'Sublime'.

Areta Greek 'Of excellent virtue'.
Arete, Aretha, Aretta, Arette, Retha

Arethusa Greek 'Virtuous'.

Arezou Persian 'Wishful'.

Argenta Latin 'Silvery one'.
Argente, Argentia

Aria Latin 'Beautiful melody'.

Ariadne Greek 'Holy one'.
Ariadna, Ariane

Arianwen Welsh 'Silvery one'.

Ariella Hebrew 'God's lioness'.
Ariel, Arielle

Arilda German 'Hearth, home'.

Arista Greek 'The best'.

Arlene Celtic 'A pledge'.
Arlana, Arleas, Arleen, Arlen, Arlena, Arletta, Arlette, Arlina, Arline, Arlyne, Herleva

Armilla Latin 'Bracelet'.
Armillette

Armina Teutonic 'Warrior maid'.
Armine, Arminia, Erminia, Erminie

Arpita Sanskrit 'Dedicated'.

Arselma Norse 'Divine protective helmet'.

Artemisia Greek/Spanish 'Perfect'.

Aruna Sanskrit 'Sunrise', 'reddish-brown'.
Aruni, Arunima

Arvinda   Sanskrit 'Lotus blossom'.
Arabinda

Asha   Sanskrit 'Hope, desire'.

Ashanti   Swahili From the West African tribe.

Ashima   Sanskrit 'Without limit'.
Aseema

Ashira   Hebrew 'Wealthy'.

Ashley   Old English 'From the ash tree meadow'.

Ashlyn   English 'Pool by the ash tree'.

Ashna   Sanskrit 'Friend'.

Asia   Greek 'Ressurrection'.

Aspasia   Greek 'Welcome' or 'radiant'.

Aspen   English 'Aspen tree'.

Assunta   Italian 'From the Assumption (of Mary)'.
Assumpta

Asta   Greek 'Star-like'.
Astera, Astra, Astrea

Atara   Hebrew 'Crown'.

Athalia   Hebrew 'God is exalted'.
Atalia, Athalea, Athalie, Athie, Attie

Athena   Greek The Greek goddess.
Athene, Athenee

Audrey   Anglo-Saxon 'Strong and noble'.
Audie, Audrie, Audry, Dee

Aura   Latin 'Gentle breeze'.
Aure, Auria, Ora

Aurelia Latin 'Golden'. The girl of the dawn.
Aurea, Aurel, Aurelie, Aurie, Auristela, Aurora, Aurore, Ora, Oralia, Oralie, Oriel, Oriole

Autumn Latin Season.

Avel Hebrew 'Breath'.

Aveline Hebrew 'Pleasant'.

Avena Latin 'Oatfield'. A girl with rich, golden hair.
Avene

Avenida Chilean 'An avenue'.

Avice French 'War-like'.
Avisa, Hadwisa

Avicia German 'Refuge in war'.

Avonwy Welsh 'Someone who lives by the river'.

Awel Welsh 'Gentle breeze'.

Awena Welsh 'Poetry, prophecy'.

Aya Hebrew 'Swift flyer'.

Ayala Hebrew 'Deer'.

Ayanna Hindi 'Innocent one'.

Ayesha Persian 'Happy one'.

Ayla Hebrew 'Oak tree'.

Aylwen Welsh 'Fair brow'.

Azalea Latin 'Dry earth'. From the flower of the same name.
Azalee, Azalia, Azaliea

Azura French 'The blue sky'. One whose eyes are blue.

girls

B

Badryah — Arabic 'Full moon'.

Bailey — French 'Steward'.

Bala — Sanskrit 'Girl'.

Balbina — Latin 'She who hesitates'.

Bambi — Latin 'The child'.

Baptista — Latin 'Baptized'.
Baptiste, Batista, Battista

Barbara — Latin 'Beautiful stranger'.
Bab, Babb, Babe, Babette, Babs, Babita, Barb, Barbetta, Barbie, Barbra, Bas

Barrie — Gaelic 'Markswoman'.

Basilia — Greek 'Queenly, regal'. Feminine of Basil.

Basima — Arabic 'Smiling'.

Bathilda — Teutonic 'Battle commander'.

Bathsheba	Hebrew 'Seventh daughter'. *Batsheva*
Beata	Latin 'Blessed, divine one'. *Bea*
Beatrice	Latin 'She who brings joy'. *Bea, Beatrix, Bee, Beitris, Trix, Trixie, Trixy*
Bebba	Swiss from Hebrew 'God's oath'.
Bedelia	Celtic 'Mighty'. *Delia*
Behira	Hebrew 'Brilliant'.
Bela	Slavonic 'White'.
Belda	French 'Beautiful lady'.
Belicia	Spanish 'Dedicated to God'.
Belinda	Italian 'Wise and immortal beauty'. *Bella, Belle, Linda, Lindie, Lindy*
Beline	French/Old German 'Goddess'.
Belisama	Latin Roman divinity like Minerva, goddess of wisdom.
Belita	Spanish from Latin 'Beautiful'.
Bellance	Italian 'Blonde beauty'. *Blanca*
Belle	French 'Beautiful woman'. *Bell, Bella, Bellina, Belva, Belvia*
Belvina	Latin 'Fair girl'.
Benedicta	Latin 'Blessed one'. Feminine of Benedict. *Benedetta, Benecia, Benedika, Benita, Bennie, Benoite, Binnie, Dixie*

Benigna Latin 'Gentle, kind and gracious'.

Benilda Latin 'Well-intentioned'.

Benita Spanish 'Blessed'.
Benitia

Berdine Teutonic 'Glorious one'.

Bernadette French 'Brave as a bear'.
Berna, Bernadene, Bernadina, Bernadine, Bernardina, Berneta, Berney, Bernie, Bernita,

Bernessa Teutonic 'With the heart of a bear'.

Bernia Latin 'Angel in armour'.
Bernie

Bernice Greek 'Herald of victory'.
Berenice, Berny, Bunny, Burnice, Veronica

Berthelda Teutonic 'Girl who goes into battle'.

Beryl Greek 'Precious jewel'. This stone, and therefore the name, is said to bring good luck.
Beril, Berri, Berrie, Berry, Beryle

Bethany Aramaic 'House of poverty'.
Bethena, Bethina

Bethel Hebrew 'House of God'.
Beth

Bethia Hebrew 'Daughter of God'.

Bethseda Hebrew 'House of Mercy'.
Bethesda

Beverley Anglo-Saxon 'Ambitious one'.
Berry, Bev, Beverlie, Beverly

Bevin Celtic 'Melodious lady'.
Bebhinn, Bethinn

Bianca Italian 'White'.

Bienvenida Spanish 'Welcome'.

Bijou Old French 'Jewel'.

Billie Teutonic 'Wise, resolute ruler'.
Billy, Billye, Willa

Bina African 'To dance'.
Binah

Birdie Modern English 'Sweet little bird'.

Blaine Gaelic 'Thin'.
Blane, Blayne

Blair Gaelic 'Dweller on the plain'.
Blaire

Blake Old English 'Fair haired'.
Blakelee, Blakeley

Blanche French 'Fair and white'.
Bellanca, Blanca, Blanch, Blanka, Blinne, Blinnie, Bluinse, Branca

Blanda Latin 'Seductive, flattering, caressing'.
Blandina, Blandine

Blasia Latin 'She who stammers'.
Blaise

Blondelle French 'Little fair one'.
Blondie

Blossom Old English 'Fragrant as a flower'.

Bo Chinese 'Precious'.

Bodgana Polish 'God's gift'.

Bonita Latin 'Sweet and good'.
Bona, Bonne, Bonnibelle, Bonnie, Nita

Bradley Old English 'From the broad meadow'.
Bradlee, Bradleigh

Brandy Dutch 'Brandy'.
Brandais, Brandea, Brandice

Branwen Welsh 'Beautiful raven'.

Breanna Irish 'Strong and honourable'.
Breana, Breann, Breanne, Breighann

Brenna Irish 'Raven-haired beauty'.

Briallen Welsh 'Primrose'.

Briana Celtic 'Strength, virtue, honour'.
Breona, Bria, Brianna, Brienne, Briona, Bryana

Briar French 'Heather'.
Brier

Bridget Irish/Celtic 'Strong and mighty'.
*Biddie, Biddy, Birkita, Breita, Bridey, Bridie, Brie, Brieta,
Brietta, Brigette, Brigid, Brigida, Brigitte, Brita, Brydie*

Brittany Latin 'Britain'.
Britannia, Britney, Britta

Bronwen Welsh/Celtic 'White bosomed'.
Bronwyn

Bronya Russian 'Armour'.

Brook Old English 'Living near the brook'.
Brooke

Brooklyn American Place name.

Brucie French 'From the thicket'. Feminine of Bruce.

Brunella Italian 'One with brown hair.' The true brunette.
Bruella, Bruelle, Brunelle

Brunhilda Teutonic 'Warrior heroine'.
Bronhilde, Brunhild, Brunhilde

Bryna Irish 'Strength with virtue'. Feminine of Brian.
Brina

Bryony Old English 'A twining vine.'
Briony

Buena Spanish 'The good one'.
Buona

Bunny English 'Little rabbit'.

Burnetta French 'Little brown one'.

Cachet French 'Desirous'.
Cachée

Cadence Latin 'Rhythmic'.
Cadena, Cadenza

Caera Gaelic 'Spear, ruddy'.

Cai Vietnamese 'Feminine'.
Cae, Cay, Caye

Caitlin Gaelic 'Pure girl'. Form of Catherine.

Cala Arabic 'Castle'.

Calandra Greek 'Lark.' One who is as light as a bird.
Cal, Calandre, Calandria, Callie, Cally

Calantha Greek 'Beautiful blossom'.
Cal, Calanthe, Callie, Cally, Kalantha, Kalanthe

Caldora Greek 'Beautiful present'.

Caledonia	Latin 'Scottish lassie'. *Caledonie*
Calida	Spanish 'Ardently loving'.
Calista	Greek 'Most beautiful of women'. *Calisto, Callista, Kallista, Kallisto*
Calla	Greek 'Beautiful'. *Calli*
Callena	Teutonic 'One who talks a lot'.
Callidora	Greek 'Gift of beauty'.
Calligenia	Greek 'Daughter of beauty'.
Calliope	Greek 'The music of poetry'.
Callula	Latin 'Little beautiful one'.
Calosa	Greek 'Beautiful to look at'.
Caltha	Latin 'Yellow flower'.
Calvina	Latin 'Bald'. Feminine of Calvin.
Calypso	Greek 'Concealer'. *Kalypso*
Cam	Vietnamese 'Sweet citrus fruit'.
Cameo	Italian 'Sculptured jewel'.
Camilla	Latin 'Noble and righteous'. *Cam, Camala, Camelia, Camella, Camellia, Camile, Camille, Cammi*
Canace	Latin 'The daughter of the wind'. *Kanaka, Kanake*
Candace	Latin 'Pure, glittering, brilliant white'. *Candice, Candida, Candie, Candy*

Candra Latin 'Luminescent'.

Caprice Italian 'Fanciful'.
Capriccia

Cara Celtic/Italian 'Friend' (Celtic) or 'Dearest one' (Italian).
Caralie, Cariad, Carina, Carine, Kara, Karine, Karina

Caragh Irish 'Love'.

Cari Turkish 'Flows like water'.

Carina Latin 'Keel'.
Karina

Carissa Latin 'Most dear one'.
Caressa, Caresse, Carisse

Carita Latin 'Beloved little one'.
Karita

Carma Sanskrit 'Destiny'. From the Buddhist 'Karma' – Fate.

Carmel Hebrew 'God's fruitful vineyard'.
Carma, Carmela, Carmelina, Carmeline, Carmelita, Carmella, Carmie, Melina

Carmen Latin 'Songstress'. One who has a beautiful voice.
Carma, Carmacita, Carmelita, Carmencita, Carmia, Carmina, Carmine, Carmita, Charmaine

Caroline Teutonic 'Little woman, born to command'.
Carey, Carilla, Carly, Carlin, Carline, Caro, Carol, Carola, Carole, Carolina, Carolyn, Caryn, Charleen, Charlene, Charlotte

Caronwen Welsh 'Little fair love'.

Caryl Welsh 'Beloved'.
Carryl, Carys

Casilda   Spanish 'The solitary one'.
Casilde

Casimira   Latin 'Bringer of peace'.

Cassandra   Greek Prophetess ignored by men.
Cass, Cassandre, Cassie, Kassandra

Cassia   Greek 'Spicy cinnamon'.

Cassidy   Irish 'Clever'.

Cassiopeia   Greek 'Scent of flowers'.

Casta   Latin 'Of pure upbringing'.
Caste

Catherine   Greek 'Pure maiden'.
Caireen, Caitlin, Caitrin, Carine, Caryn, Catalina, Caterina, Catharina, Catharine, Cathelle, Cathie, Cathleen, Cathy, Catriona, Kaitlyn, Kate, Katerine, Kateryn, Katie, Katharina, Katharine, Katherina, Katherine, Kathryn, Kathy, Katrina, Katrine, Katy, Kit, Kitty

Cathlin   Celtic 'One with beautiful eyes'.

Catriona   Scottish 'Pure maiden'. Scottish variation of Catherine.

Cattima   Latin 'Delicate reed'.

Cayla   Hebrew 'Crown of laurel leaves'.
Kayla, Caily

Ceara   Irish 'Spear'.

Cecilia   Latin The patron saint of music.
Cecelia, Cecil, Cecile, Cecily, Cele, Celia, Cicely, Ciel, Cissie, Sheila, Sileas, Sisile, Sisle, Sisley, Sissie

Cedrella   Latin 'Silver fir tree'.

Ceinlys   Welsh 'Sweet gems'.

Ceinwen Welsh 'Beautiful gems'.

Ceiridwen Welsh The goddess of bardism.
Ceri, Kerridwen

Celandine Greek 'Swallow' or 'yellow water flower'.
Celandon

Celeste Latin 'Heavenly'.
Cele, Celesta, Celestina, Celestine, Celestyna, Celia, Celina, Celinda, Celinka

Celo Greek 'Flame-like'.

Celosia Greek 'Burning flame'.
Kelosia

Cerelia Latin 'Spring-like'.
Cerealia, Cerelie, Cerellia

Cerian Welsh 'Loved one'.

Ceridwen Welsh 'Fair poetry'.
Ceri

Cerrita Spanish 'Closed, silent'.

Cerys Welsh 'Love'.

Chakra Sanskrit 'Circle of energy'.
Chakara, Shakra

Champa Sanskrit 'Flower'.
Champak

Chan Cambodian 'Sweet-smelling tree'.

Chandni Sanskrit 'Moonlight'.

Chandra Sanskrit 'The moon who outshines the stars'.
Candra, Candre, Chandre

Chanel	Old French 'Wine jar'.
Chantelle	French 'Little singer'. *Chantal, Chantel*
Chantesuta	Native American 'Resolute'.
Charis	Greek 'Grace'.
Charity	Latin 'Benevolent and loving'.
Charlotte	Teutonic A form of Caroline. *Carla, Carlie, Carly, Carlotta, Charlie, Charlotta, Charmian, Charo, Charyl, Cheryl, Sharleen, Sherry, Sheryl*
Charma	Greek 'Delight'.
Charmaine	Latin 'Little song'. *Carmen, Charmain, Charmian*
Charmian	Greek 'Little joy'.
Chastity	Latin 'Purity'.
Chatura	Sanskrit 'Clever one'.
Chelsea	Old English 'A port of ships'. *Chelsey, Chelsy, Cheslie, Kelsie*
Chenoa	Native American 'White bird'.
Cherie	French 'Dear, beloved one'. *Cheri, Cherida, Cherry, Cheryl, Sherrie, Sherry, Sheryl*
Cherise	Old French 'Cherry-like'.
Cheron	French 'Beloved'. *Caron*
Chesna	Slavic 'Peaceful'.
Cheyenne	American Tribal name.

Chiara Italian 'Famous, light'.

Chika Japanese 'Near, thousand rejoicings'.

Chilali Native American 'Snow bird'.

Chimalis Native American 'Blue bird'.

Chiquita Spanish 'Little one'.

Chitsa Native American 'Beautiful one'.

Chloe Greek 'Fresh young blossom'. Also Chlöe.
Cloe, Kloe

Chlora Greek 'Spring freshness'.

Chloris Greek 'Goddess of the flowers'.
Chloras, Chlores, Chlori, Loris

Cho Japanese 'Butterfly'.

Cholena Native American 'Bird'.

Christabel Latin 'Beautiful bright-faced Christian'.
Christabella, Christabelle, Kristabel, Kristabella, Kristabelle

Christanta Colombian 'A chrysanthemum'.

Christine French 'Christian one'.
*Cairistiona, Cairstine, Chris, Chrissie, Chrissy, Christan,
Christian, Christiana, Christiane, Christina, Christye,
Crystal, Kristen, Krystina, Tina*

Chryseis Latin 'Golden daughter'.

Chrysilla Greek 'One with golden hair'.

Chun Chinese 'Springtime'.

Cilla French 'The cilla flower'.

Cinderella	French 'Girl of the ashes'. From the fairy tale. *Cindie, Cindy, Ella*
Clairine	Latin 'Bright maiden'.
Clanenda	Latin 'Becoming brighter'.
Clara	Latin 'Bright, shining girl'. *Claire, Clare, Clareta, Clarette, Clarine, Klara*
Claramae	English 'Brilliant beauty'. *Chlarinda, Chlorinda, Clarinda, Clorinda*
Claresta	English 'The most shining one'. *Clarista*
Claribel	Latin 'Fair and bright'.
Clarice	French 'Little, shining one'. French form of Clara. *Chlaris, Clariss, Clarissa, Clarisse*
Clarimond	Teutonic 'Brilliant protector'. *Chlarimonda, Chlarimonde, Clarimonda, Clarimonde*
Claudia	Latin 'The lame one'. Feminine of Claud. *Claude, Claudell, Claudette, Claudie, Claudina, Claudine, Gladys*
Clearesta	Greek 'Pinnacle of achievement'.
Clematis	Greek 'Sweet wine'.
Clemence	Latin 'Merciful and kind'. *Clemency, Clementia, Clementina, Clementine*
Cleopatra	Greek 'Her father's glory'. *Cleo*
Cleophila	Greek 'Lover of glory'.
Cleosa	Greek 'Famous'.

Cleva Old English 'Cliff dweller'. Feminine of Clive.

Cliantha Greek 'Flower of glory'.
Cleantha, Cleanthe, Clianthe

Clio Greek 'She who proclaims'.

Clodagh Irish A river in Ireland.

Clorinda Latin 'Famed for her beauty'.
Chlorinda, Chlorinde, Clarinda, Clarinde, Clorinde

Clotilda Teutonic 'Famous battle maiden'.
Clothilda, Clothilde, Clotilde

Clover English 'Meadow blossom'.
Clovie

Clydina Greek 'Glorious'.

Clymene Greek 'Fame and renown'.

Clytie Greek 'Splendid daughter'.

Cocheta Native American 'Unknown one'.

Cody Old English 'A cushion'.

Colette Latin 'Victorious'.
Collete, Collette

Colinette Latin 'Tiny dove'.

Comfort French 'One who gives comfort'.

Conception Latin 'Beginning'.
Concepcion, Conceptia, Concha, Conchita

Concessa Latin 'One who grants a favour'.

Concetta Italian 'An ingenious thought'.

Concordia Latin 'Harmony and Peace'.
Concordie, Concordina, Concordy

Connal	Latin 'Faithful one'.
Conradine	Teutonic 'Bold and wise'. Feminine of Conrad. *Connie, Conrada, Conradina*
Consolata	Latin 'One who consoles'. *Consolation*
Consuela	Spanish 'Consolation'. A friend in need. *Connie, Consuelo*
Cora	Greek 'The maiden'. *Corella, Corett, Corette, Corin, Corina, Corinna, Corinne, Correna, Coretta, Corie, Corrie, Corrina*
Corabella	Combination Cora/Bella 'Beautiful maiden'. *Corabelle*
Coral	Latin 'Sincere' or 'From the sea'. *Corale, Coralie, Coraline*
Corazon	Spanish 'Heart'.
Cordelia	Welsh 'Jewel of the sea'. *Cordelie, Cordie, Cordula, Delia*
Corey	Gaelic 'From the hollow'.
Corissa	Latin/Greek 'Most modest maiden'. *Corisse*
Corla	Old English 'Curlew'.
Corliss	English 'Cheerful and kind-hearted'. *Carliss, Carlissa, Corlissa*
Cornelia	Latin 'Womanly virtue'. *Cornela, Cornelie, Cornelle, Cornie, Nela, Nelie, Nelli*
Corolla	Latin 'Tiny crown'.

Corona Spanish 'Crowned maiden'.
Coronie

Cosette French 'Victorious army'.
Cosetta

Cosina Greek 'World harmony'.
Cosima

Coulava Celtic 'One with soft hands'.

Courtney Old English 'From the court'.
Courtenay

Coyetta Teutonic 'Caged'.

Coyne French 'Modest'.

Crescent French 'The creative one'.
Crescenta, Crescentia

Cressida Greek 'The golden one'.
Cresseide

Crispina Latin 'Curly haired'. Feminine of Crispin.
Crispine

Crystal Latin 'Clear'.
Christalle, Cristal, Chrystal, Krystal

Cynara Greek 'Artichoke'. A beautiful maiden, protected by thorns.

Cynthia Greek 'Moon goddess'.
Cindy, Cyn, Cynth, Cynthie

Cyra Persian 'The sun god'.

Cyrena Greek 'From Cyrene'.
Cyrenia, Kyrena, Kyrenia

Cyrilla Latin 'Lordly one'. Feminine of Cyril.
Cirila, Cirilla

girls

Dacey Gaelic 'Southerner'.

Dacia Greek 'From Dacia'.

Daffodil Greek 'Golden spring flower'.

Dagania Hebrew 'Ceremonial grain'.

Dagmar Norse 'Glory of the Danes'.

Dahlia Greek 'Of the valley'.

Dai Japanese 'Great'.

Daisy Anglo-Saxon 'The day's eye'. Also a nickname for Margaret (Marguerite), French for daisy.

Dakapaki Native American 'Blossom'.

Dakota American 'Friend, partner'. Tribal name.

Dale Teutonic 'From the valley'.
Dael, Daile

Dallas Gaelic 'Wise'.

Dalta Gaelic 'Favourite child'.

Damara Greek 'Gentle girl'.
Damaris, Mara, Maris

Damasa French 'Maiden'.

Damia Greek 'Goddess of forces of nature'.

Damita Spanish 'Little noble lady'.

Dana Scandinavian 'From Denmark'.
Dayna

Danae Greek Mother of Perseus.

Danica Norse 'The morning star'.
Danika

Danielle Hebrew 'God is my judge'. Feminine of Daniel.
*Danella, Danelle, Danice, Daniela, Danielea, Danila, Danita,
Danya, Danyelle*

Danuta Polish 'Young deer'.

Daphne Greek 'Bay tree'. Symbol of victory.

Dara Hebrew 'Charity, compassion and wisdom'.
Darya

Daraka Sanskrit 'Gentle and shy'.

Daralis Old English 'Beloved'.

Darcie French 'From the fortress'. Feminine of D'Arcy.
D'Arcie

Darcy Celtic 'Girl with dark hair'.
Darcia, Dercia, Dercy

Darel Anglo-Saxon 'Little dear one'. Another form of Darlene.
Darelle, Darrelle, Darry, Daryl

D
girls

Daria Greek 'Wealthy queen'. Feminine of Darius.

Darice Persian 'Queenly'.
Dareece, Darees

Darlene Anglo-Saxon 'Little darling'.
Darea, Dareen, Daria, Darleen, Darline, Daryl

Daron Gaelic 'Great'.

Dasha Russian 'Gift of God'.

Davina Hebrew 'Beloved'. Feminine of David
Daveen, Davida, Davita

Dawn Anglo-Saxon 'The break of day'.

Dea Latin 'Goddess'.

Deborah Hebrew 'The bee'. An industrious woman.
Debbie, Debby, Debor, Debora, Debra, Devora

Dee Welsh 'Black, dark'.

Deiphila Greek 'Divine love'.

Deirdre Gaelic 'Sorrow'. A legendary Irish beauty.
Deerdre, Deidre

Deja French 'Before'.

Delfine Greek 'The larkspur or delphinium flower'.
Delfina, Delphina, Delphine, Delveen

Delia Greek 'Visible'. Another name for the Moon goddess.

Delicia Latin 'Delightful maiden'. 'Spirit of delight'.

Delie French 'Slim and delicate'.

Delight French 'Pleasure'.

Delilah Hebrew 'The gentle temptress'.
Dalila, Delila, Lila

Delinda	Teutonic 'Gentle'.
Delma	Spanish 'Of the sea'. *Delmar, Delmare*
Delora	Latin 'From the seashore'. *Dellora*
Delphine	Greek 'Calmness and serenity'.
Delta	Greek 'Fourth daughter'.
Delwen	Welsh 'Neat, fair'.
Delyth	Welsh 'Neat, pretty'.
Demelza	English 'Hill-fort'.
Demetria	Greek 'Fertility'. *Demi, Demeter*
Dena	Anglo-Saxon 'From the valley'. *Deana, Deane*
Denaneer	Arabic 'Piece of gold'.
Denise	French 'Wine goddess'. Feminine of Dionysus, God of wine. *Denice, Denny, Denys*
Derryth	Welsh 'Of the oak'.
Desdemona	Greek 'One born under an unlucky star'.
Desiree	French 'Desired one'.
Desma	Greek 'A pledge'.
Destinee	Old French 'Destiny'.
Deva	Sanskrit 'Divine'. The Moon goddess.
Devi	Hindu Name of a Hindu goddess.

Devin Gaelic 'Poet'.

Devnet Celtic 'White wave'.

Devona English 'From Devon'.
Devondra

Diamanta French 'Diamond-like'.

Diamond Latin 'Precious jewel'.

Diana Latin 'Divine Moon goddess'.
Deanna, Dee, Di, Diahann, Dian, Diandra, Diane, Dianna, Dianne, Dyana, Dyane, Dyanna

Diantha Greek 'Divine flower of Zeus'.
Dianthe, Dianthia

Didi Hebrew 'Beloved'.

Didiane French Feminine of Didier.
Didière

Diella Latin 'One who worships God'.

Dilys Welsh 'Perfect'.

Dinah Hebrew 'Judgement'.

Dione Greek 'The daughter of heaven and earth'.
Dionia, Dionne

Disa Norse 'Lively spirit'.

Disa Greek 'Double'.

Divya Hindi 'Divine, heavenly'.
Divia

Dixie French 'The tenth'.
Dixey, Dixil, Dixy

Docila Latin 'Gentle teacher'.

Dodie Hebrew 'Beloved'.

Dolores Spanish 'Lady of Sorrow'.
Delora, Delores, Deloris, Delorita, Dolly, Doloritas, Lola, Lolita

Domina Latin 'The lady'. One of noble birth.

Dominica Latin 'Child born on a Sunday'.

Dominica Latin 'Belonging to the Lord'. Feminine of Dominic.
Domenica, Domeniga, Dominga, Domini, Dominique

Donabella Spanish 'Beautiful woman'.

Donalda Gaelic 'Ruler of the world'. Feminine of Donald.

Donata Latin 'The gift'.

Donella Spanish 'Little girl'.

Donna Italian 'Noble lady'.
Dona

Dorcas Greek 'Graceful'.

Dore French 'Golden maiden'.

Dorea Greek 'Gift'.

Doreen Gaelic 'Golden girl', alternatively 'the sullen one'.
Dora, Dorene, Dori, Dorie, Dori, Dorie, Dorine, Dory

Dorhissa Hebrew 'Gift of the promise'.

Dorianne Greek 'From Doria'.

Dorinda Greek/Spanish 'Beautiful golden gift'.

Doris Greek 'From the sea'. The daughter of Oceanus.
Dodi, Dora, Dorice, Dorise, Dorita, Dorris

Dorleta Basque Name for the Virgin Mary.

Dorothy Greek 'Gift of God'. A form of Theodora.
Deel, Dolley, Dollie, Dolly, Dora, Dore, Doretta, Dorothea, Dorothi, Dorothoe, Dorthea, Dot, Thea, Theodora

Dove English 'Bird of peace'.

Dromicia Greek 'Fast'.

Druella Teutonic 'Elfin vision'.
Druilla

Drusilla Latin 'The strong one'.

Duana Gaelic 'Little dark maiden'.
Duna, Dwana

Duena Spanish 'Chaperon'.
Duenna

Dulcie Latin 'Sweet and charming'.
Delcine, Dulce, Dulcea, Dulciana, Dulcibella, Dulcibelle, Dulcine, Dulcinea

Durene Latin 'The enduring one'.

Duretta Spanish 'Little reliable one'.

Duscha Russian 'Soul'.

Dyani Native American 'Deer'.

Dympna Irish 'Eligible'.
Dymphna

Dyna Greek 'Powerful'.

Dyota Sanskrit 'Sunshine'.

Dysis Greek 'Sunset'.

girls

Earlene Anglo-Saxon 'Noble woman'. Feminine of Earl.
Earley, Earlie, Earline, Erlene, Erline

Easter Old English 'Born at Easter'. The pre-Christian goddess of spring.
Eastre, Eostre

Eberta Teutonic 'Brilliant'.

Ebony Greek 'A hard, dark wood'.

Echo Greek 'Repeating sound'.

Eda Greek/Anglo-Saxon 'Loving mother of many', 'prosperous' (Greek) or 'poetry' (Anglo-Saxon).
Eada, Edda

Edana Gaelic 'Little fiery one'.
Aidan, Aiden, Eidann

Eden Hebrew 'Enchanting'. The epitome of all female charm.

Edia Teutonic 'Rich friend'.

E
girls

Edina   Scottish Another form of Edwina.

Edith   Teutonic 'Rich gift'.
Eadie, Eadith, Eaidie, Eady, Eda, Edythe, Ede, Edie, Editha, Edithe, Ediva

Edlyn   Anglo-Saxon 'Noble maiden'.

Edmee   Anglo-Saxon 'Fortunate protector'.

Edmonda   Anglo-Saxon 'Rich protector'. Feminine of Edmund.
Edmunda

Edna   Hebrew 'Rejuvenation'.
Ed, Eddie, Edny

Edra   Hebrew 'Mighty'.

Edrea   Anglo-Saxon 'Powerful and prosperous'. Feminine of Edric.
Eadrea

Edwina   Anglo-Saxon 'Rich friend'.
Eadwina, Eadwine, Edina, Edwine, Win, Wina, Winnie

Effie   Greek 'Famous beauty'.
Effy

Eglatine   French 'Wild rose'.

Eiblin   Gaelic 'Pleasant'.
Eveleen

Eilien   Greek 'Light'.

Eilwen   Welsh 'Fair brow'.

Eir   Norse 'Peace and mercy'. The goddess of healing.

Eirian   Welsh 'Silver'.

Eirlys   Welsh 'Snowdrop'.

Eirwen   Welsh 'Snow-white'.

Ekata Sanskrit 'Unity'.

Elaine French French form of Helen.
Lainey

Elama Greek 'From the mountains'.

Elana Hebrew 'Oak tree'.

Elata Latin 'Lofty, noble'.

Elberta Teutonic 'Brilliant'.

Elda Anglo-Saxon 'Princess'.

Eldrida Teutonic 'Old and wise adviser'. Feminine of Eldred.
Aeldrida

Eleanor French A medieval form of Helen.
Eleanora, Eleanore, Elinor, Elinora, Elinore, Eleonor,
Eleonora, Eleonore, Ellie, Lenora, Leonora, Nora

Electra Greek 'Brilliant one'.

Elga Slav 'Consecrated'.
Olga

Elinel Celtic 'Shapely'.

Eliora Hebrew 'God is my light'.
Eleora

Elita Old French 'Chosen'.

Elizabeth Hebrew 'Consecrated to God'.
Bess, Bessie, Bessy, Beth, Betina, Betsy, Betta, Bette,
Betty, Elisa, Elisabeth, Elise, Elissa, Eliza, Eloise, Elsbeth,
Else, Elsie, Ilse, Libby, Lisa, Liza, Lizzy and all the forms of
Isabel

Ella Teutonic 'Beautiful fairy maiden'.

Ellenis Greek 'Priestess'.

Ellice Greek 'Jehovah is God'. Feminine of Elias.
Ellis

Ellora Greek 'Happy one'.

Elma Greek 'Pleasant and amiable'.

Elmina Old German 'Awe-inspiring fame'.

Elodie Greek 'Fragile flower'.

Eloine Latin 'Worthy to be chosen'.

Eloise French 'Noble one'. Also a form of Elizabeth.

Elora Greek 'Light'.

Elrica Teutonic 'Ruler of all'.
Ulrica

Elsa Old German 'Noble'.

Elswyth Old English 'Noble strength'.

Elva Anglo-Saxon Friend of the elves'.
Elfie, Elvia, Elvie, Ivina

Elvina Teutonic 'Wise and friendly'.

Elvira Latin 'White woman'.
Albinia, Alinia, Elvera, Elvire, Elwira

Elvita Latin 'Life'.

Elwy Welsh 'Benefit'.

Elwyn Welsh 'One with brown hair'.

Elysia Latin 'Blissful sweetness'. From Elysium.
Elicia, Elise

Emanuela Hebrew 'God is with you'.

Embla Scandinavian The first woman in Norse mythology.

Emer Irish 'Gifted'.

Emerald French 'The bright green jewel'.
Emerande, Emerant, Eneraude, Esme, Esmeralda, Esmeralde

Emily Teutonic 'Hard working'.

Emina Latin 'Highly born maiden'.

Emma Teutonic 'One who heals the universe'.
Ema, Emelina, Emeline, Emmeline

Emmanuela Hebrew 'God with us'.

Emmeranne French/Old German 'Raven'.

Emrys Celtic 'Immortal'.
Emryss

Ena Gaelic 'Little ardent one'. Also dimunitive of Eugenia.

Enda Sanskrit 'The last one'.

Endocia Greek 'Of spotless reputation'.
Docie, Doxie, Doxy, Eudosia, Eudoxia

Endora French/Old German 'Noble'.

Enfys Welsh 'Rainbow'.

Engelberta Teutonic 'Bright angel'. One of the bright defenders of legend.
Engelberga, Engelbert, Engelbertha, Engelberthe

Engracia Spanish 'Graceful'.

Ennata French/Greek 'Goddess'.

Enona Greek Nymph of Mount Ida, who married Paris.

Enone Greek 'Flower in the hedgerow'.

Enora French/Greek 'Light'.

Enrica Italian Italian form of Henrietta.

Enya Irish 'Kernel'.

Ephratah Hebrew 'Fruitful'.

Eranthe Greek 'Flower of spring'.

Erica Norse 'Powerful ruler'. Symbol of royalty.
Aric, Erika

Erin Gaelic 'From Ireland'.

Erina Gaelic 'Girl from Ireland'.

Erlina Old English 'Little elf'.

Erma Teutonic 'Army maid'.
Ermina, Erminia, Erminie, Hermia, Hermina, Hermione

Ernestine Anglo-Saxon 'Purposeful one'.
Ernesta

Erwina Anglo-Saxon 'Friend from the sea'.

Esha Sanskrit 'One who desires'.
Eshita

Essylt Welsh 'Beautiful to behold'.

Esta Italian 'From the East'.

Estaphania Greek 'Crown'.

Estelle French 'Bright star'.
Estella, Estrelita, Estrella, Stella, Stelle

Esther Hebrew 'The star'.
Eister, Essa, Etty, Hessy, Hester, Hesther, Hetty

Etain Irish 'Shining'.

Ethel Teutonic 'Noble maiden'.
Ethelda, Etheline, Ethyl, Ethylyn

Ethelinda Teutonic 'Noble serpent'. The symbol of immortality.

Etoile French 'Star'.

Eudora Greek 'Generous gift'.
Dora, Eudora

Eudosia Greek 'Esteemed'.
Eudocia

Eugenia Greek 'Well born'. A woman of noble family.
Ena, Eugenie, Gena, Gene, Genie, Gina

Eulalia Greek 'Fair spoken one'.
Eula, Eulalie, Lallie

Euphemia Greek 'Of good reputation'.
Effie, Effy, Euphemie, Phemie

Eurielle Celtic/French 'Angel'.

Evadne Greek 'Fortunate'.

Evangeline Greek 'Bearer of glad tidings'.
Eva, Evangelina, Vancy, Vangie

Evania Greek 'Tranquil, untroubled'.
Evanne

Evanthe Greek 'Lovely flower'.

Eve Hebrew 'Life giver'.
Eva, Eveleen, Evelina, Eveline, Evelyn, Evie, Evita, Evonne

Evie Popular variation of Eve.

Evodie Greek 'One who follows the right path'.

Ezara Hebrew 'Little treasure'.

Fabia Latin 'Bean grower'.
Fabiana Fabianna, Fabienne

Fabiola Latin 'Woman who does good works'.

Fabrianne Latin 'Girl of resourcefulness'.
Fabrianna, Fabrienne, Frabriane

Fadilla French Diminutive of Françoise (see Frances).

Faida Arabic 'Abundant'.

Faith Teutonic 'Trust in God'. One who is loyal and true.
Fae, Fay, Faye

Fallon Gaelic 'Grandchild of the ruler'.

Fanchon French 'Free being'. A derivative of Françoise (see Frances).

Fania Teutonic 'Free'.

Fanshom Teutonic 'Free'.

Farha Sanskrit 'Happiness'.
Farhad, Farhat

Farhanna Arabic 'Joyful'.

Farica Teutonic 'Peaceful rule'.

Farida Arabic 'Unique, precious gem'.

Farideh Persian 'Glorious'.

Fariha Arabic 'Happy'.

Farrah Middle English 'Beautiful'.
Farah

Faten Arabic 'Fascinating, charming'.

Fathia Arabic 'My conquest'.

Fatima Arabic 'Unknown'.

Fausta Italian/Spanish 'Fortunate'.

Faustine Latin 'Lucky omen'.
Fausta, Faustina

Favor French 'The helpful one'.
Favora

Fawn French 'Young deer'. A lithe, swift-footed girl.
Faun, Faunia, Fawnia

Fay Irish 'A raven'.
Fae, Faye, Fayette, Fayina

Fayre Old English 'Beautiful'.

Felda Teutonic 'From the field'. For one born at harvest time.

Felicia Latin 'Joyous one'. Feminine of Felix.
Felice, Felicidad, Felicie, Felicity, Felis, Felise, Feliza

Felipa Greek 'One who loves horses'.

Felita Latin 'Happy little one'.

Fenella Gaelic 'White shouldered'.
Finella, Fionnula

Feride Turkish 'Unique'.

Feriga Italian/Teutonic 'Peaceful ruler'.

Fern Anglo-Saxon 'Fern-like'.

Fernanda Teutonic 'Adventurous'. One who is daring and courageous.
Ferdinanda, Fernandina

Feronia Latin A goddess of the forests'.

Ffion Welsh 'Foxglove flower'.

Fidela Latin 'Faithful one'.
Fidele, Fidelia, Fidelity

Filma Anglo-Saxon 'Misty veil'. An ethereal type of beauty.
Philmen, Pholma

Finette Hebrew 'Little addition'.

Fingal Celtic 'Beautiful stranger'.

Finley Gaelic 'Sunbeam'.

Finna Celtic 'White'.

Fiona Gaelic 'Fair one'.
Fionn, Fionna

Flanna Gaelic 'Red-haired'.

Flavia Latin 'Yellow haired'.

Fleta Anglo-Saxon 'The swift one'.
Fleda

Fleur French 'A flower'. French version of Florence.
Fleurette

Fleurdelice French 'Iris or lily'.

Florence Latin 'A flower'.
Fiora, Firoenza, Fleur, Flo, Flor, Flora, Florance, Flore,
Florella, Florencia, Florentia, Florenza, Floria, Florinda,
Florine, Floris, Florrie, Florry, Flossie, Flower

Florette French 'Little flower'.
Floretta

Florida Latin 'Flowery'.

Florimel Greek 'Flower honey'.

Flower English The English version of Florence.

Fonda English 'Affectionate'.

Fontanna French 'Fountain'.

Fortune Latin 'Fate'. The woman of destiny.
Fortuna

Fossetta French 'Dimpled'.

Frances Latin 'Free' or 'Girl from France'.
Fan, Fanny, Fran, Francesca, Francine, Francisca,
Franciska, Françoise, Frankie

Freda Teutonic 'Peace'. One who is calm and unflurried.
Freddie, Freida, Frida, Frieda, Friedie

Frederica Teutonic 'Peaceful ruler'.
Farica, Freddie, Freddy, Fredericka, Frederika, Frederique,
Frerika, Frerike, Friederik

Fredicia Teutonic 'Peaceful leader'.

Fresa Teutonic 'One with curly hair'.

Freya Norse 'Noble goddess of love'.

Frodine Teutonic 'Wise companion'.

Froma Teutonic 'Holy one'.

Fronde Latin 'Fern leaf'.

Fulca Latin 'Accomplished'.

Fulvia Latin 'Golden girl'. Born at high summer.

Gabinia French/Italian from Latin Famous Roman family; city in central Italy

Gabrielle Hebrew 'Woman of God'. The bringer of good news.
Gabbie, Gabriel, Gabriela, Gabriele, Gabriella, Gabrila, Gaby, Gavrielle

Gaea Greek 'The earth'. The goddess of the Earth.
Gaia

Gaerwen Welsh 'White castle'.

Galatea Greek 'Milky white'.

Galia Hebrew 'God has redeemed'.

Galiena Teutonic 'Lofty maiden'.
Galiana

Galilah Hebrew Place name in Galiliee.

Gardenia Latin 'White, fragrant flower'.

Garland French 'Crown of blossoms'.

Garnet	English 'Deep-red-haired beauty'. *Garnette*
Gaviota	Spanish 'Seagull'.
Gavra	Hebrew 'God is my rock'.
Gavrila	Hebrew 'Heroine'.
Gay	French 'Lively'. *Gai, Gaye*
Gazella	Latin 'The antelope'. One who is graceful and modest.
Gedalia	Hebrew 'God is great'.
Geena	Sanskrit 'Silvery'.
Geeta	Sanskrit The holy book of advice from Lord Krishna to Arjuna.
Gelasia	Greek 'Laughing water'. *Gelasie*
Gemini	Greek 'Twin'.
Gemma	Latin 'Precious stone'. *Gemmel*
Genesia	Latin 'Newcomer'. *Genesa, Genisia, Jenesia*
Geneva	French 'Juniper tree'. Also variation of Genevieve. *Genevre, Genvra, Ginerva*
Genevieve	French 'Pure white wave'. *Gaynor, Geneva, Genevra, Genevre, Genovera, Ginette, Ginevra, Guenevere, Guinevere, Jennifer, Jenny*
Georgia	Greek 'Farm girl'. Also a form of Georgina.
Georgina	Greek 'Girl from the farm'. Feminine of George. *Georgana, Georganne, Georgene, Georgette, Georgia, Georgiana, Georgianna, Georgie*

Geraldine Teutonic 'Noble spear carrier'.
Geralda, Geraldina, Gerhardine, Geri, Gerianna, Gerrilee,
Gerry, Giralda, Jeraldine, Jeri, Jerri, Jerry

Geranium Greek 'Bright red flower'.

Gerda Norse 'Protected one'.
Garda

Germaine French 'From Germany'.
Germain

Gertrude Teutonic 'Spear maiden'. One of the Valkyrie.
Gartred, Gerda, Gert, Gertie, Gertrud, Gertruda, Gertrudis,
Gerty, Trudie, Trudy

Gervaise French from Teutonic 'Eager for battle'.

Gianina Hebrew 'The Lord's grace'.

Gilah Hebrew 'Joy'.

Gilberta Teutonic 'Bright pledge'. Feminine of Gilbert.
Gigi, Gilberte, Gilbertha, Gilberthe, Gilbertina, Gilbertine,
Gillie, Gilly

Gilda Celtic 'God's servant'.

Gillian Latin 'Young nestling'. Also derivative of Juliana (see Julia).
Gill, Gillie, Jill, Jillian, Jillie

Giselle Teutonic 'A promise'.
Gisela, Gisele, Gisella, Gizela

Gita Hindi 'Song'.

Gitana Spanish 'The gypsy'.

Gittle Hebrew 'Innocent flatterer'.
Gytle

Gladys Celtic 'Frail delicate flower'. Celtic version of Claudia (the lame).
Glad, Gladdie, Gladine, Gladis, Gleda, Gwladys, Gwyladys

Gleda Anglo-Saxon Old English version of Gladys.

Glenna Celtic 'From the valley'.
Glenda, Glenine, Glenn, Glennis, Glynis

Glenys Welsh 'Holy'.

Glinys Welsh 'Little valley'.

Gloria Latin 'Glorious one'.
Gloire, Glori, Gloriana, Gloriane, Glorianna, Glorianne, Glory

Godine Teutonic 'Friend of God'.

Godiva Anglo-Saxon 'Gift of God'.
Godgifu

Goldie Anglo-Saxon 'Pure gold'.
Golda, Goldina

Gondoline Teutonic 'Brave and wise'.

Goneril Latin 'Honoured'.

Gorvena Teutonic 'One who lives in the forest'.

Grace Latin 'The graceful one'.
Engacia, Engracia, Giorsal, Gracia, Gracie, Gratiana, Grayce, Grazia

Gracienne Latin 'Small one'.

Graciosa Spanish 'Graceful and beautiful'.

Graine Celtic 'Love'.

Grainne Irish 'Love'.
Grania

Grazina Italian 'Grace, charm'.

Gredel   Teutonic 'Pearl'.

Greer   Greek 'The watchful mother'.
Gregoria

Grimonia   Latin 'Wise old woman'.

Griselda   Teutonic 'Grey heroine'.
Griselde, Grishelda, Grishelde, Grishilda, Grishilde, Grizelda, Selda, Zelda

Guadalupe   Arabic 'River of black stones'.

Guda   Anglo-Saxon 'The good one'.
Goda

Gudila   Teutonic 'God is my help'.

Gudrid   Teutonic 'Divine impluse'.

Gudrun   German 'War, rune'.

Guida   Latin 'The guide'.

Guinèvere   Celtic 'White phantom'.
Gaynor, Ginerva, Guenna, Guinivere, Guenevere, Gwenhwyvar, Jennifer

Gundred   Teutonic 'Courageous and wise'.

Gunhilda   Norse 'Warrior maid'.
Gunhilde

Gustava   Scandinavian 'Staff of the Goths'.
Gussie, Gussy, Gustave

Gwendoline   Celtic 'White-browed maid'.
Guenna, Gwenda, Gwendolen, Gwendolene, Gwendolyn, Gwendolyne, Gwen, Gwennie, Gwyn, Wendy

Gwendydd   Welsh 'Morning star'.

Gweneal	Celtic	'White angel'.
Gweneira	Welsh	'White snow'.
Gwenllian	Welsh	'Fair, Flaxen'.
Gwennol	Welsh	'Swallow'.
Gwenonwyn	Welsh	'Lily of the valley'.
Gwylfai	Welsh	'May festival'.
Gwyneth	Welsh	'Blessed'.
Gwynne	Celtic	'White' or 'fair one'.
Gyda	Teutonic	'Gift'.
Gypsy	Anglo-Saxon	'The wanderer'.
	Gipsy	

girls

H

Habiba	Sanskrit 'Beloved'.
Hafwen	Welsh 'Summer-beautiful'.
Hagar	Hebrew 'Forsaken'.
Haidee	Greek 'Modest, honoured'.
Halcyone	Greek 'The kingfisher'. *Halcyon*
Haley	Scandinavian 'Hero'. *Haleigh*
Halima	Arabic 'Kind, humane'.
Halimeda	Greek 'Sea thoughts'. One who is drawn to the sea. *Hallie, Meda*
Halla	African 'Unexpected gift'.
Hallie	Greek 'Thinking of the sea'. *Halette, Hali, Halley*
Halona	Native American 'Fortunate'.

Hana Japanese 'Flower'.
Hanako

Hannah Hebrew 'Full of grace'.

Hanusia Hebrew 'Grace of the Lord'.

Happy English 'Happy'.

Harmony Latin 'Concord and harmony'.
Harmonia, Harmonie

Harshada Sanskrit 'Joy bringer'.

Harshita Sanskrit 'Happy'.
Harshini

Haru Japanese 'Springtime'.

Hasina Sanskrit 'Beautiful one'.

Hasita Sanskrit 'Laughing one'.

Hasna Arabic 'Beautiful'.

Hatsu Japanese 'First-born'.

Hayfa Arabic 'Slender'.

Hayley English From the surname.
Hailey, Haylie

Hazar Arabic 'Nightingale'.

Hazel English 'The hazel tree'.
Aveline

Heather Anglo-Saxon 'Flower of the moors'.

Hebe Greek Goddess of youth.

Hedda Teutonic 'War'. A born fighter.
Heddi, Heddy, Hedy

Hedia Greek 'Pleasing'.

Hedwig Teutonic 'Safe place in time of trouble'.

Heera Sanskrit 'Diamond'.

Heidi Teutonic 'Noble and kind'. Popular form of Adalheid.

Helbona Hebrew 'Fruitful'.

Helen Greek 'Light'.
Aileen, Aisleen, Alleen, Eileen, Elaine, Elane, Eleanor, Elena, Elenora, Ella, Ellen, Galina, Helena, Helene, Lana, Lena, Leonora, Nell, Nora

Helga Teutonic 'Pious, religious and holy'. Variation of Olga.

Helia Greek 'Sun'.

Helianthe Greek 'Bright flower; sunflower'.

Helice Greek 'Spiral'.
Helixa

Helma Teutonic 'A helmet'
Hilma

Helonia Greek 'Marsh lily'.

Helvitia Latin 'Home on the hill'.

Henrietta Teutonic 'Ruler of home and estate'. Feminine of Henry.
Eiric, Enrica, Etta, Harriet, Harriette, Harriot, Harriotte, Hattie, Hatty, Henriette, Hendrika, Henrika, Hetty, Minette, Netta, Yetta

Hera Latin 'Queen of the heaven'.

Hermione Greek 'Of the earth'. Daughter of Helen of Troy.
Hermia, Hermina, Hermine, Herminia

Hermosa Spanish 'Beautiful'.

Hernanda Spanish 'Adventuring life'.

Hero Greek Mythological lover of Leander.

Hesper Greek 'The evening star'.
Hespera, Hesperia

Hestia Greek 'A star'.

Heutte Old English 'Brilliant'.
Huetta, Hugette, Hughette

Hiberna Latin 'Girl from Ireland'.
Hibernia

Hibiscus Latin 'The marshmallow plant'.

Hidé Japanese 'Excellent, fruitful, superior'.

Hilary Latin 'Cheerful one'. One who is always happy.
Hilaire, Hilaria

Hilda Teutonic 'Battle maid'.
Heidi, Heidy, Hidie, Hild, Hilde, Hildie, Hildy

Hina Hebrew 'Female deer'.

Hippolyta Greek 'Horse destruction'.

Holly Anglo-Saxon 'Bringer of good luck'.
Hollie

Honesta Latin 'Honourable'.

Honey English 'Sweet one'.

Honora Latin 'Honour'.
Honey, Honor, Honoria, Honour, Nora, Norah, Noreen, Norine, Norrey, Norrie, Norry

Hope Anglo-Saxon 'Cheerful optimism'.

Horatia Latin 'Keeper of the hours'. Feminine of Horace.
Haracia, Horacia

Hoshi Japanese 'Star'.

Howin Chinese 'Loyal swallow'.

Huberta Teutonic 'Brilliant maid'.
Hubertha, Huberthe

Huette Anglo-Saxon 'Brilliant thinker'. Feminine of Hugh.
Huetta, Hugette

Hyacinth Greek 'Hyacinth flower'.
Cynthie, Cynthis, Giacinta, Hyacintha, Hyacinthia, Jacinda, Jacinth Jacintha, Jacinthia, Jackie

Ianira   Greek 'Enchantress'.

Ianthe   Greek 'Violet-coloured flower'.
Ian, Iantha, Ianthina, Janthina, Janthine

Ida   Teutonic 'Happy'.
Idalina, Idaline, Idalle, Idelea, Idella, Idelle

Idalia   Spanish 'Sunny'.

Idmonia   Greek 'Skilful'.

Iduna   Norse 'Lover'. The keeper of the golden apples of youth.
Idonia, Idonie

Ierne   Latin 'From Ireland'.

Ignatia   Latin 'Fiery ardour'. Feminine of Ignatius.
Ignacia

Ignes   Latin 'Pure'.

Ila   French 'From the island'.
Ilde

Ilana Hebrew 'Tree'.

Ileana Greek 'Of Ilion (Troy)'.

Ilka Slavic 'Flattering'.

Iluminada Spanish 'Illuminated'.

Imelda Latin 'Wishful'.
Imalda, Melda

Immaculada Spanish 'Immaculate conception'.

Imogene Latin 'Image of her mother'.
Imogen

Imperial Latin 'Imperial one'.
Imperia

India Hindi 'From India'.

Indira Hindi 'Beauty' or 'splendid'.

Ingrid Norse 'Hero's daughter'. Child of a warrior.
Inga, Ingaberg, Ingeborg, Ingebiorg, Inger, Ingibiorg, Ingunna

Iniga Latin 'Fiery ardour'.
Ignatia

Intisar Arabic 'Triumph'.

Iola Greek 'Colour of the dawn cloud'.
Iole

Iolanthe Greek 'Violet flower'.
Yolanda, Yolande

Ione Greek 'Violet-coloured stone'.
Iona

Irene Greek 'Peace'. The goddess of peace.
Eirena, Eirene, Erena, Irena, Irenna, Irina, Rena, Renata, Rene, Reini, Rennie, Renny

Ireta Latin 'Enraged one'.
Irete, Iretta, Irette

Iris Greek 'The rainbow'. The messenger of the Gods.
Irisa

Irma Teutonic/Latin 'Strong' or 'noble'.
Erma, Erme, Irmina, Irmine, Irme

Irvette English 'Sea friend'.
Irvetta

Isa Teutonic 'Lady of the iron will'. A determined girl.

Isabel Hebrew Spanish form of Elizabeth.
Bel, Bella, Belle, Isabeau, Isabella, Isabelle, Isobel and the variations of Elizabeth

Isabella Popular variation of Isabel.

Isabelle Popular variation of Isabel.

Isadora Greek 'The gift of Isis'.
Dora, Dori, Dory, Isadore, Isidora, Isidore, Issie, Issy, Izzy

Isis Egyptian 'Supreme goddess'. The goddess of fertility.

Isla Latin/French 'Island'.

Islamey Arabic 'Obedient to Allah'.

Ismena Greek 'Learned'.

Isola Latin 'The isolated one'. A loner.

Isolabella Combination Isola/Bella 'Beautiful lonely one'.
Isolabelle

Isolde Celtic 'The fair one'.
Esyllt, Iseult, Isoda, Yseult, Ysolda, Ysolde

Iva French 'The yew tree'.
Ivanna, Ivanne

Iverna Latin An old name for Ireland.

Ivory Welsh 'Highborn lady'.

Ivy English 'A vine'. The sacred plant of the ancient religions.

Izora Arab 'Dawn'.

girls

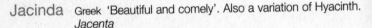

Jacinda Greek 'Beautiful and comely'. Also a variation of Hyacinth.
Jacenta

Jacoba Latin 'The supplanter'.
Jacobina, Jacobine

Jacqueline Hebrew 'The supplanter'.
Jacketta, Jackie, Jacklyn, Jacky, Jacobina, Jacqueleine, Jacquelyn, Jacquetta, Jacqui, Jamesina, Jaquith

Jade Spanish 'Daughter'. A mother's most precious jewel.
Jada

Jaffa Hebrew 'Beautiful'.

Jagoda Slavonic 'Strawberry'.

Jahola Hebrew 'Dove'.

Jaime French 'I love'.
Jaimee, Jaimey, Jamey, Jamie, Jaymee

Jala Arabic 'Clarity'.

Jalaya Sanskrit 'Lotus blossom'.

Jalila Arabic 'Great'.

Jamila Muslim 'Beautiful'.

Jamuna Sanskrit 'Holy river'.

Jane Hebrew 'God's gift of grace'.
Jan, Jana, Janet, Janette, Janetta, Janice, Janina, Janna, Jayne, Jaynell, Jean, Jeanette, Jeanne, Joan, Joanna, Joanne, Juanita, Nita, Sean, Seonaid, Sheena, Siân, Sinead, Siobhan

Janet Hebrew 'God's gift of grace'. A variation of Jane.

Jarita Hindi 'Legendary bird'.

Jarmila Slavic 'Spring'.

Jarvia Teutonic 'Keen as a spear'.

Jasmine Persian 'Fragrant flower'.
Jasmin, Jasmina, Jessamie, Jessamine, Jessamy, Jessamyn, Yasmin, Yasmina, Yasmie

Jawahir Arabic 'Jewels'.

Jayati Sanskrit 'Victorious'.
Jayata

Jayne Sanskrit 'God's victorious smile'. Also a variation of Jane.

Jeanette Hebrew 'God's gift of grace'. A variation of Jane.

Jelena Greek 'Light'.

Jemina Hebrew 'The dove'. Symbol of peace.
Jemie, Jemmie, Mina

Jena Arabic 'A small bird'.
Genna, Jenna

Jennifer English 'White phantom'. A variation of the Celtic Guinèvere.
Jenni, Jenny

Jeremia Hebrew 'The Lord's exalted'. Feminine of Jeremiah.
Jeri, Jerrie, Jerry

Jessica Hebrew 'The rich one'.
Jessalyn

Jessie Hebrew 'God's grace'.

Jevera Hebrew 'Life'.

Jewel Latin 'Most precious one'. The ornament of the home.

Jinx Latin 'Charming spell'.
Jynx

Joakima Hebrew 'The Lord's judge'.
Joachima

Jobina Hebrew 'The afflicted'. Feminine of Job.
Jobyna

Joby Hebrew 'Persecuted'. A feminine form of Job.

Jocasta Greek 'Shining moon'.

Joccoaa Latin 'The humorous one'. Girl with a lively wit.

Jocelyn Latin 'Fair and just'. Feminine of Justin.
*Jocelin, Joceline, Jocelyne, Joscelin, Josceline, Joscelyn,
Joscelyne, Joselen, Joselene, Joselin, Joseline, Joselyn,
Joselyne, Josilen, Josilene, Josilin, Josiline, Josilyn,
Josilyne, Joslin, Josline, Justina, Justine, Lyn, Lynne*

Jocunda Latin 'Full of happiness'.

Jodette Latin 'Active and sporty'.

Joelle Hebrew 'The Lord is willing'.

Jolene Middle English 'He will increase'.
Joleen, Jolyn

Jolie French 'Pretty'.
Jolee, Joly

Joliette French 'Violet'.
Joletta

Jonquil Latin From the name of the flower.

Jordana Hebrew 'The descending'.
Jordan

Josephine Hebrew 'She shall add'. Feminine of Joseph.
*Fifi, Jo, Joette, Josepha, Josephina, Josetta, Josette,
Josie, Pepita, Yosepha, Yusepha*

Jovita Latin 'The joyful one'.

Joyce Latin 'Gay and joyful'.
Joice, Joicelin, Joicelyn, Joy, Joycelin, Joycelyn, Joyous

Juanita Spanish 'God's gift of grace'.

Judith Hebrew 'Admired, praised'.
Jodie, Jody, Judie, Juditha, Judy, Siobhan, Siuban

Julia Greek 'Youthful'.
*Jill, Juli, Juliana, Juliane, Julianna, Julianne, Julie, Juliet,
Julietta, Julina, Juline, Sile, Sileas*

Jumanah Arabic 'Pearl'.

Jun Chinese 'Truthful'.

June Latin 'Summer's child'.
Juana, Juna, Junia, Juniata, Junette, Junine

Junko Japanese 'Obedient'.

Juno Latin 'Heavenly being'.

Jurisa Slavonic 'Storm'.

Jutta Latin 'Near'.

Jyoti Hindi 'Light'.

Jyotsna Sanskrit 'Moonlight'.

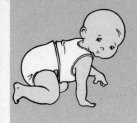

Kabira — Arabic 'Powerful'.

Kachina — Native American 'Sacred dance'.

Kagami — Japanese 'Mirror'.

Kairos — Greek 'Goddess born last to Jupiter'.

Kala — Hindi 'Black, time'.

Kalama — Native American 'Wild goose'.

Kalamit — Hebrew 'Flower'.

Kali — Sanskrit 'Energy'.

Kalika — Sanskrit 'A bud'.

Kalila — Arabic 'Beloved'.
Kally, Kaylee, Kylila

Kalma — Teutonic 'Calm'.

Kalonice — Greek 'Beauty's victory'.

Kalwa — Finnish 'Heroic'.

Kalya   Sanskrit 'Healthy'.

Kalyana   Sanskrit 'Virtuous one'.

Kalyca   Greek 'Rosebud'.

Kama   Sanskrit 'Love'. The Hindu god of love, like Cupid.

Kamama   Native American 'Butterfly'.

Kamana   Sanskrit 'Desire'.

Kameko   Japanese 'Child of the tortoise'. The tortoise is a symbol of long life.

Kamilah   Arabic 'The perfect one'.
Kamila

Kamra   Arabic 'Moon'.

Kanakabati   Sanskrit 'Fairy-tale princess'.

Kanya   Thai 'Young lady'.

Karabel   Spanish 'Lovely face'.

Karma   Sanskrit 'Destiny'.

Kasia   Greek 'Pure'.

Katherine   Greek 'Pure maiden'.
Kara, Karen, Karena, Karin, Karyn, Kate, Katharina, Katharine, Katherina, Katheryn, Kathie, Kathleen, Kathryn, Katie, Katrina, Kay, Kitty and all variations of Catherine

Kaumudi   Sanskrit 'Moonlight'.

Kayla   Hebrew 'Crown'.

Kayleigh   Modern from Arabic 'Beloved'. Modern name derived from Kalila.

Keely   Gaelic 'The beautiful one'

Kelda   Norse 'Bubbling spring'.
Kelly

Kelly   Irish Gaelic 'Warrior maid'.
Kellina

Kelsey   Scandinavian 'From the island of the ships'.
Kelci, Kelsi, Kesley

Kendra   Old English 'Knowledgeable'.
Kenna

Keren   Hebrew 'Horn of antimony'.

Kerry   Gaelic 'Dark one'.
Kerri, Kerrianne

Keshena   Native American 'Swift in flight'.

Keshina   Sanskrit 'Girl with beautiful hair'.

Kesia   African 'Favourite'.

Ketura   Hebrew 'Incense'.

Keyne   Celtic 'Jewel'.

Khalida   Arabic 'Immortal, everlasting'.

Khalipha   Arabic 'Successor'.

Kiah   African 'Season's beginning'.

Kim   Origin not known 'Noble chief'.

Kimberley   English 'From the royal meadow'.
Kimberlyn, Kimbra

Kina   Greek 'Christian'.

Kineta   Greek 'Active and elusive'.

Kinnereth   Hebrew 'From the Sea of Galilee'.

Kiona Native American 'Brown hills'.

Kira Persian 'Sun'.

Kirby Old English 'From the church town'.
Kirbee, Kirbie

Kirima Eskimo 'A hill'.

Kirstin Norse 'The annointed one'.
Kirsten, Kirstie, Kirstina, Kirsty, Kirstyn

Kohana Japanese 'Little flower'.

Kolfinna Celtic 'Cool, white lady'.

Kolina Greek 'Pure'.

Kolotosa Native American 'Star'.

Komala Sanskrit 'Charming, tender'.
Komal

Kora Greek 'Young girl, maiden'.
Korella, Koressa

Koren Greek 'Beautiful maiden'.

Kotsasi Native American 'White flower'.

Krishna Sanskrit Hindu god.

Kuki Japanese 'Snow'.

Kuni Japanese 'Born in the countryside'.

Kuntala Sanskrit 'Girl with beautiful hair'.
Kuntal

Kurva Japanese 'Mulberry tree'.

Kwai Chinese 'Rose-scented'.

Kyla Gaelic 'Pretty one'.
Kilah, Kylah, Kylie

La Roux French 'The red-haired one'.
Larousse, Roux

Labiba Arabic 'Wise'.

Lada Russian 'Mythological goddess of beauty'.

Ladonna French 'The lady'.

Lala Slavic 'The tulip flower'.

Lalage Greek 'Gentle laughter'.

Lalana Sanskrit 'Beautiful one'.
Lalan

Laleh Persian 'Tulip'.

Lalita Sanskrit 'Beautiful', 'without guile'.
Lalit

Lalota Sanskrit 'Pleasing'.

Lamya Arabic 'Dark lips'.

Lane	Middle English 'From the narrow road'.
Lanelle	Old French 'From the little lane'.
Lani	Hawaiian 'The sky'.
Lara	Latin 'Famous'.
Larentia	Latin 'Foster mother'. *Laurentia*
Larine	Latin 'Girl of the sea'. *Lareena, Larene, Larianna*
Larissa	Greek 'Cheerful maiden'. *Lacee, Lacey, Laris*
Lark	English 'Singing bird'.
Lasca	Latin 'Weary one'.
Lassie	Scottish 'Little girl'.
Latonia	Latin 'Belonging to Latona'. *Latona, Latoya*
Laura	Latin 'Laurel wreath'. *Laure, Laureen, Laurel, Lauren, Laurena, Laurene, Lauretta, Laurette, Laurie, Lora, Loralie, Lorenza, Loretta, Lorna*
Lauren	Latin 'Laurel wreath'. Familiar form of Laura.
Laveda	Latin 'One who is purified'. *Lavetta, Lavette*
Lavelle	Latin 'Cleansing'.
Lavena	Celtic 'Joy'.
Lavender	English 'Sweet-smelling flower'. *Lavvie*

Laverne French 'Spring-like' or 'Alder tree'.
Laverna, Vern, Verna, Verne

Lavinia Latin 'Lady of Rome'.
Lavina, Vina, Vinia

Layla Arabic 'Night'.
Laila

Leah Hebrew 'The weary one'.
Lea, Lee, Leigh

Leala French 'The true one'.

Leandra Latin 'Like a lioness'.
Leodora, Leoline, Leonelle

Leatrice Hebrew 'Tired but joyful'. Combination of Leah and Beatrice.
Leatrix

Lechsinska Polish ''Woodland spirit'.

Leda Greek 'Mother of beauty'. The mother of Helen of Troy.

Lee English 'From the fields'. Also a variation of Leah.
Leanna, Leeann

Leena Sanskrit 'Devoted one.'

Lefa Teutonic 'The heart of the tree'.

Leigh Old English 'From the meadow'.

Leilani Hawaiian 'Heavenly blossom'.
Lillani, Lullani

Lemma Ethiopian 'Developed'.

Lemuela Hebrew 'Dedicated to God'.
Lemuella

Lena   Latin 'Enchanting one'.
Lenette, Lina

Lenis   Latin 'Smooth and white as the lily'.
Lene, Leneta, Lenita, Lenta, Lenos

Lentula   Celtic 'Gentle one'.

Leocadia   Spanish from Greek 'Lion-like'.

Leoda   Teutonic 'Woman of the people'.
Leola, Leota

Leoma   Anglo-Saxon 'Bright light'.

Leona   Latin 'The lioness'.
Lennie, Lenny, Leola, Leone, Leonelle, Leoni, Leonie

Leonarda   French 'Like a lion'.
Leonarde, Leonardina, Leonardine

Leontine   Latin 'Like a lion'.
Leontina, Leontyne

Leor   Hebrew 'I have light'.

Leora   Greek 'Light'.

Lesham   Hebrew 'Precious stone'.

Lesley   Celtic 'Keeper of the grey fort'.
Les, Lesli, Leslie, Lesly

Letha   Greek 'Sweet oblivion'.
Leda, Leta, Leithia, Lethia, Lethitha

Letitia   Latin 'Joyous gladness'.
Laetitia, Leda, Leshia, Leta, Leticia, Letisha, Letizia, Lettice, Lettie, Loutitia, Tish

Levina   English 'A bright flash'.

Lewanna Hebrew 'As pure as the white moon'.
Luanna

Leya Spanish 'Loyalty to the law'.

Leyla Turkish 'Born at night'.

Lian Chinese 'The graceful willow'.

Liana French 'The climbing vine'.
Leana, Leane, Leanna, Lianna, Lianne

Liberata Latin 'Freed'.

Libusa Russian 'Beloved'.

Lida Slavic 'Beloved of the people'.

Lilac Persian 'Dark mauve flower'.

Lilian Latin 'A lily'. One who is pure.
Lela, Lelah, Lelia, Leila, Lila, Lilah, Lilais, Lili, Lilia, Liliana, Liliane, Lilias, Lilla, Lilli, Lillian, Lily

Lilith Arabic 'Woman of the night'.

Lin Chinese 'Beautiful jade'.

Linda Spanish 'Pretty one'. Also diminutive of Belinda, Rosalinda, etc.
Lind, Linde, Lindie, Lindy, Lynd, Lynda

Lindsay Old English 'From the linden tree island'.
Lindsey

Ling Chinese 'Delicate' or 'dainty'.

Linnea Norse 'The lime blossom'.
Lynnea

Linnet French 'Sweet bird'.
Linetta, Linette, Linnetta, Linnette, Lynette, Lynnette

Liorah Hebrew 'I have light'.

Liria Greek 'Tender one.'

Lisa Hebrew 'Consecrated to God'. A variation of Elizabeth or Melissa.

Lisandra Greek Feminine variation of Alexander.

Lisha Arabic 'The darkness before midnight'.
Lishe

Liyna Arabic 'Tender'.

Llawela Welsh 'Like a ruler'.
Llawella

Logan Celtic 'Little hollow'.

Loietu Native American 'Flower'.

Lola Spanish 'Strong woman'.
Loleta, Lolita, Lollie, Lulita

Lomasi Native American 'Pretty flower'.

Lona Anglo-Spanish 'Solitary watcher'.

Lorelei Teutonic 'Siren of the river'.
Lorelia, Lorelie, Lurleen

Lorelle Latin/Old German 'Little'.

Lorraine French/Teutonic 'The Queen' (French) or 'renowned in battle (Teutonic).
Larina, Larine, Laraine, Larayne, Larraine, Loraine

Lotus Greek 'Flower of the sacred Nile'.

Louella Teutonic 'Shrewd in battle'.

Louise Teutonic 'Famous battle maid'.
*Alison, Allison, Aloisa, Aloisia, Aloysia, Eloisa, Eloise,
Heloise, Labhaoise, Liusade, Lois, Louisa*

Love English 'Tender affection'.

Loveday English 'Reconciliation'.

Lowena English 'Joy'.

Luana Teutonic 'Graceful army maiden'.
Luane, Louanna, Louanne, Luwana, Luwanna, Luwanne

Luba Russian 'Love'.
Lubmila

Lucretia Latin 'A rich reward'.
Lucrece, Lucrecia, Lucrezia

Lucy Latin 'Light'.
*Lacinia, Lucette, Lucia, Luciana, Lucida, Lucie, Lucile,
Lucille, Lucinda, Lucita, Luighseach, Luisadh*

Ludella Anglo-Saxon 'Pixie maid'.

Ludmilla Slavic 'Beloved of the people'.
Ludmila

Luella Anglo-Saxon 'The appeaser'.
Loella, Louella, Luelle

Lulu Arabic 'Pearl'.

Luneda Celtic 'With a beautiful figure'.

Lunetta Latin 'Little Moon'.
Luna, Luneta

Lupe Spanish 'She wolf'. A fierce guardian of the home.

Luvena Latin 'Little beloved one'.

Lycoris Greek 'Twilight'.

Lydia Greek 'Cultured one'.
Lidia, Lidie, Lydie

Lynette English 'Idol'.
Linnet, Lyn, Lynn, Lynne

Lynn Celtic 'A waterfall'. Also diminutive of Carolyn, Evelyn, etc.
Lynne

Lyonelle Old French 'Young lion'.

Lysandra Greek 'The Liberator'. The prototype of Women's Lib!

girls

Mab Gaelic 'Mirthful joy'.
Mave, Mavis, Meave

Mabel Latin 'Amiable and loving'. An endearing companion.
Mable, Maible, Maybelle, Moibeal

Mackenzie Gaelic 'Handsome'.

Madeline Greek 'Tower of strength'.
*Mada, Madalaine, Madaleine, Madalena, Madaline,
Maddalena, Maddalene, Maddy, Madeleine, Magdalene,
Marleen, Melina*

Madhulika Sanskrit 'Honey'.

Madhur Hindi/Sanskrit 'Sweet'.
Madhura, Madhuri

Madison Teutonic 'Child of Maud'.

Madra Spanish 'The matriarch'.

Maeve Irish The warrior queen of Connaught.
Mave, Meave

Magaski Native American 'White swan'.

Magdi Arabic 'My glory'.

Magnolia Latin 'Magnolia flower'.
Mag, Maggie, Nola, Nolie

Maha Arabic 'Wild oxen'.

Mahala Hebrew Tenderness'.
Mahalah, Mahalia

Maida Anglo-Saxon 'The maiden'.
Mady, Maidel, Maidie, Mayda, Mayde, Maydena

Majesta Latin 'Majestic one'.

Malika Sanskrit 'Garland of flowers'.

Malise Gaelic 'Servant of God'.

Mallika Sanskrit 'Jasmine flower'.

Mallory French 'Unlucky'.

Malva Greek 'Soft and tender'.
Melba, Melva

Malvina Gaelic 'Polished chieftain'.
Malva, Malvie, Melva, Melvina, Melvine

Manuela Spanish 'God with us'.
Manuella

Marcella Latin 'Belonging to Mars'.
Marcela, Marcelia, Marcelle, Marcelline, Marchella, Marchelle, Marchelline, Marchita, Marcia, Marcie, Marsha

Marelda Teutonic 'Famous battle maiden'.

Mareria Latin 'Of the sea'.
Maralla

Margaret Latin 'A pearl'.
Daisy, Greta, Grete, Gretchen, Grethe, Maggie,
Maigrghread, Maisie, Margalo, Margarita, Marge, Margorie,
Margot, Marguerite, Meg, Peggy, Rita

Marian Hebrew 'Bitter and graceful'.
Mariam, Mariana, Marianna, Marianne, Mariom, Marion,
Maryanne

Marigold English 'Golden flower girl'.
Marygold

Marina Latin 'Lady of the sea'.
Marnie

Mariposa Spanish 'Butterfly'.

Maris Latin 'Of the sea'.
Marisa, Marissa, Marris

Marola Latin 'Woman who lives by the sea' or 'little dark girl'.

Martha Arabic 'The mistress'.
Marta, Martella, Marthe, Marti, Martie, Martita, Marty,
Martynne, Mattie, Matty

Martina Latin 'War-like one'. Feminine of Martin.
Marta, Martine, Tina

Marvel Latin 'A wondrous miracle'.
Marva, Marvela, Marvella, Marvelle

Mary Hebrew 'Bitterness'.
Mamie, Manette, Marette, Maria, Mariah, Marie, Mariel,
Marietta, Marilyn, Maureen, May, Miriam, Mitzi, Molly, Polly

Maryam Arabic 'Purity'.

Masa Japanese 'Straightforward, upright'.

Massa Arabic 'Uplifting'.

Massima　Italian/Latin 'Greatest'.

Mathilda　Teutonic 'Brave little maid'.
Maitilde, Matelda, Mathilde, Matilda, Matilde, Mattie, Tilda, Tilly

Matsu　Japanese 'Pine tree'.

Mattea　Hebrew 'Gift of God'. Feminine of Matthew.
Mathea, Mathia, Matthea, Matthia

Maud　Teutonic 'Brave girl'.

Maurilla　Latin 'Sympathetic woman'.
Mauralia, Maurilia

Mauve　Latin 'Lilac-coloured bird'.
Malva

Mavis　French 'Song thrush'.

Maxine　French 'The greatest'. Feminine of Maximilian.
Maxene, Maxie, Maxima

May　Latin 'Born in May'. Also dimunitive of Mary.
Maia, May

Maya　Sanskrit 'Illusion'.

Mead　Greek 'Honey wine'.
Meade

Meara　Gaelic 'Mirth'.

Medea　Greek 'The middle child' or 'Enchantress'.
Madora, Media, Medora

Medora　Literary Poetic character of Lord Byron.

Medwenna　Welsh 'Maiden, princess'.
Modwen, Modwenna

Megan Celtic 'The strong one'.
Meagan, Meaghan, Meghan, Meghann

Megar Greek First wife of Hercules.

Meinwen Welsh 'Slim'.

Meiying Chinese 'Beautiful flower'.
Mei

Melada Greek 'Honey'.

Melanie Greek 'Clad in darkness'.
Malan, Mel, Melan, Melania, Melany, Mellie, Melloney, Melly

Melantha Greek 'Dark flower'.
Melanthe

Melina Latin 'Yellow canary'. Also derivative of Madeline.

Melinda Greek 'Mild and gentle'.
Malinda

Melior Latin 'Better'.

Melissa Greek 'Honey bee'. 'Nymph of the forest'.
Lisa, Lissa, Mel, Melisa

Melita Greek 'Little honey flower'.
Elita, Malita, Melitta

Melle Celtic/French 'Princess'.

Melody Greek 'Like a song'.
Lodie, Melodia, Melodie

Mercedes Spanish 'Compassionate, merciful'.
Merci, Mercy

Mercia Anglo-Saxon 'Lady of Mercia'.

Mercy Middle English 'Compassion, mercy'.

Meredith   Celtic 'Protector from the sea'.
Meredeth, Meredydd, Meredyth, Merideth, Meridith, Meridyth, Merrie, Merry

Merle   Latin 'The blackbird'.
Merl, Merla, Merlina, Merline, Merola, Meryl, Myrlene

Merlyn   Celtic/Spanish 'Sea hill'.
Merlina

Merrie   Anglo-Saxon 'Mirthful, joyous'. Also diminutive of Meredith.
Meri, Merri, Merry

Merrila   Greek 'Fragrant'.

Merrilees   Old English 'St. Mary's field'.
Merrilie

Merritt   Anglo-Saxon 'Worthy, of merit'.
Meritt, Meritta, Merrit, Merritta

Merula   Latin 'Blackbird'.

Messina   Latin 'The middle child'.

Meta   Latin 'Ambition achieved'.

Metea   Greek 'Gentle'.

Metis   Greek 'Wisdom and skill'.
Metys

Mevena   Celtic/French 'Agile'.

Mia   Latin 'Mine'.

Michaela   Hebrew 'Likeness to God'. Feminine of Michael.
Micaela, Michaelina, Michaeline, Michaella, Michel, Micheline, Michella, Michelle

Michal   Hebrew 'God is perfect'.

Michi Japanese 'The way'.

Michiko Japanese 'Three thousand'.

Midori Japanese 'Green'.

Mignon French 'Little, dainty darling'.
Mignonette

Mihewi Native American 'Woman of the sun'.

Miki Japanese 'Stem'.

Mildred Anglo-Saxon 'Gentle counsellor'.
Mildrid, Milli, Millie, Milly

Millicent Teutonic 'Strong and industrious'.
Melisande, Melisandra, Milicent, Millie, Milly

Mimosa Latin 'Imitative'.

Minda Indian 'Knowledge'.

Mindora Teutonic 'Gift of love'.

Minerva Latin 'Wise, purposeful one'. The goddess of wisdom.

Minette French 'Little kitten'.
Minetta

Minna Old German 'Tender affection'.

Minta Greek/Teutonic 'Remembered with love'. From the plant.
Mina, Minda, Mindy, Minetta, Minnie

Mione Greek 'Small'.

Mira Latin 'Wonderful one'.
Mireilla, Mireille, Mirella, Mirilla, Myra, Myrilla

Mirabel Latin 'Admired for her beauty'.
Mirabella, Mirabelle

Miranda Latin 'Greatly admired'.
Randa

Mirta Greek/Spanish 'Crown of beauty'.
Mirtala, Myrta

Misty Old English 'Shrouded with mist'.

Mitra Persian 'Name of angel'.

Miya Japanese 'Temple'.

Mocita Sanskrit 'The one who is set free'.

Modana Sanskrit 'One who makes people happy'.

Modesty Latin 'Shy, modest'.
Desta, Modesta, Modeste, Modestia, Modestine

Moina Celtic 'Soft'.

Molly Hebrew 'Bitterness'. A variation of Mary.

Monica Latin 'Advice giver'.
Mona, Monca, Monika, Monique, Moyna

Mora Gaelic 'Sun'.

Morag Celtic 'Great'.
Moira, Moyra

Morgana Welsh 'From the sea shore'.
Morgan, Morgen

Morwena Welsh 'Maiden'.

Moselle Hebrew 'Taken from the water'. Feminine of Moses.
Mosella, Mozel, Mozella, Mozelle

Mosera Hebrew 'Bound to men'.

Motaza Arabic 'Proud'.

Moto Japanese 'Source'.

Moza Hebrew 'Fountain'.

Munira Arabic 'Illuminating, light'.

Muriel Celtic 'Sea bright'.
Meriel, Muire, Murielle

Musa Latin 'Song'.

Musetta French 'Child of the Muses'.
Musette

Mwynen Welsh 'Gentle'.

Mya Burmese 'Emerald'.

Myfanwy Welsh 'My rare one'.
Myvanwy

Myra Latin 'Admired'. 'Wonderful one'.

Myrna Gaelic 'Beloved'.
Merna, Mirna, Moina, Morna, Moyna

Myrtle Greek 'Victorious crown'. The hero's laurel wreath.
Mertice, Mertle, Mirle, Myrta, Myrtia, Myrtis

girls

N

Naamah Hebrew 'Pleasant, beautiful'.
Namana

Naashom Hebrew 'Enchantress'.
Nashom, Nashoma

Naava Hebrew 'Beautiful'.

Nabeela Arabic 'Noble'.
Nabila

Nabrissa French/Greek 'Peace'.

Nadine French 'Hope'.
Nada, Nadda, Nadeen, Nadia

Nadira Arabic 'Rare, precious'.

Nafisa Arabic 'Precious'.

Nahtanha Native American 'Cornflower'.

Naida Latin 'The water nymph'.
Naiada

Naima Arabic 'Contented'.

Nairne Gaelic 'From the river'.

Nalani Hawaiian 'Calmness of the heavens'.

Namah Hebrew 'Beautiful, pleasant'.
Nama

Nandelle German 'Adventuring life'.

Nandita Sanskrit 'Happy'.

Nani Hawaiian 'Beautiful'.

Naomi Hebrew 'The pleasant one'.
Naoma, Noami, Nomi, Nomie

Napea Latin 'Girl of the valley'.
Napaea, Napia

Nara English 'Nearest and dearest'. Also diminutive of Narda.

Narda Latin 'Fragrant perfume'.
Nara

Narmada Hindi 'Gives pleasure'.

Nasiba Arabic 'Love, poetry'.

Nasima Arabic 'Gentle breeze'.

Nasya Hebrew 'Miracle of God'.

Nata Sanskrit 'Dancer'.

Natalie Latin 'Born at Christmas tide'.
Nastasya, Natacha, Natala, Natale, Natalia, Natalina, Natasha, Nathalie, Natica, Natika, Nettie, Noelle

Nathania Hebrew 'Gift of God'.
Natene, Nathane, Nathene

Natsu Japanese 'Summer'.

Nayana Sanskrit 'Lovely eyes'.

Nazima Sanskrit 'Beautiful song'.

Neala Gaelic 'The champion'. Feminine of Neil.
Neale

Nebula Latin 'A cloud of mist'.

Neda Slav 'Born on Sunday'.
Nedda, Nedi

Nelda Anglo-Saxon 'Born under the elder tree'.

Nellwyn Greek 'Bright friend and companion'.

Neola Greek 'The young one'.

Neoma Greek 'The new moon'.

Nerima Greek 'From the sea'.
Nerice, Nerine, Nerissa, Nerita

Nerissa Greek 'Of the sea'.
Nerita

Nerys Welsh 'Lordly one'.

Netania Hebrew 'Gift of God'.

Neva Spanish 'As white as the moon'.
Nevada

Niamh Irish 'Brightness'.

Nicole Greek 'The people's victory'.
Nichola, Nicholina, Nickie, Nicky, Nicol, Nicola, Nicolina, Nicoline, Nikki, Nikola, Nikoletta

Nieta Spanish 'Granddaughter'.

Nigella Latin 'Black'.

Nikhita Sanskrit 'The earth'.

Nila Latin 'From the Nile'.
Nela

Nilaya Sanskrit 'Home'.

Nina Spanish 'The daughter'.
Nineta, Ninetta, Ninette

Nipha Greek 'Snowflake'.

Nirah Hebrew 'Light'.

Nisha Sanskrit 'Night'.

Nissa Scandinavian 'Friendly elf'.

Nixie Teutonic 'Water sprite'.
Nissie, Nissy

Nizana Hebrew 'Flower bud'.

Nokomis American Indian 'The grandmother'.

Nola Gaelic 'Famous one'.

Noleta Latin 'Unwilling'.
Nolita

Nona Latin 'Ninth born'.

Norberta Teutonic 'Bright heroine'.
Norberte, Norbertha, Norberthe

Nordica Teutonic 'Girl from the North'.
Nordika

Norma Latin 'A pattern or rule'.
Noreen, Normi, Normie

Norna Norse 'Destiny'. The goddess of fate.

Novia Latin 'The newcomer'.
Nova

Nuala Gaelic 'One with beautiful shoulders'.

Numidia Latin 'The traveller'.

Nydia Latin 'A refuge, nest'.

Nyssa Greek 'Starting point'.

Nyx Greek 'White haired'.

Obelia Greek 'A pointed pillar'.

Octavia Latin 'The eighth child'.
Octavie, Ottavia, Ottavie, Tavi, Tavia, Tavie, Tavy

Oda Teutonic 'Rich'.

Odelette French 'A small lyric'.
Odelet

Odelia Teutonic 'Prosperous one'.
Odele, Odelie, Odelinda, Odella, Odilia, Odilla, Otha, Othilla, Ottilie

Odessa Greek 'A long journey'.

Odette French 'Home lover'. One who makes a house a home.

Odile French/German 'Rich'.
Odeline, Odila

Ofrah Hebrew 'Young mind, lively maiden'.

Ola Scandinavian 'Descendant'. The daughter of a chief'.

O
girls

Olaathe Native American 'Beautiful'.

Olatta Native American 'Lagoon'.

Olave Teutonic 'Ancestor's relic'.

Olethea Latin 'Truth'.
Alethea, Oleta

Olga Teutonic 'Holy'.
Elga, Helga, Livi, Livia, Livie, Livvi, Olenka, Olive, Olivia, Ollie, Olva

Olien Russian 'Deer'.

Olinda Latin 'Fragrant herb'.

Olive Latin 'Symbol of peace'. Also derivative of Olga.
Livia, Nola, Nollie, Olivette, Olivia, Ollie, Olva

Olwyn Welsh 'White clover'.
Olwen

Olympia Greek 'Heavenly one'.
Olimpie, Olympe, Olympie

Onawa American Indian 'Maiden who is wide awake'.

Ondine Latin 'A wave'. The wave of water.
Ondina, Undine

Oneida Native American 'Expected'.
Onida

Opal Sanskrit 'Precious jewel'.
Opalina, Opaline

Ophelia Greek 'Wise and immortal'.
Ofelia, Ofilia, Phelia

Ora Latin 'Golden one'.
Orabel, Orabella, Orabelle

Oralee Hebrew 'My light'.
Orali, Orli

Orane French 'Rising'.

Ordelia Teutonic 'Elf's spear'.

Orea Greek 'Of the mountain'.

Orela Latin 'Divine pronouncement'.

Orella Latin 'Girl who listens'.

Orenda American Indian 'Magic power'.

Oriana Latin 'Golden one'.
Oria, Oriane

Orla Irish 'Golden lady'.

Orlena French 'Gold'.

Orna Gaelic 'Pale coloured'.

Orpah Hebrew 'A fawn'.

Orva Teutonic 'Spear friend'.

Orvala Latin 'Worthy of gold'.

Osanna Latin 'Filled with mercy'.

Ovina Latin 'Like a lamb'.

Owena Welsh 'Well born'.

Owissa Native American 'Bluebird'. The bringer of spring.

Ozora Hebrew 'Strength of the Lord'.

Paciane French from Latin 'Peace'.

Pacifica Latin 'Peaceful one'.

Paige Anglo-Saxon 'Young child'.
Page

Paka Swahili 'Kitten'.

Pakshi Sanskrit 'Bird'.
Pakhi

Pallas Greek 'Wisdom and knowledge'.

Palma Latin 'Palm tree'.
Palmer, Palmira

Paloma Spanish 'The dove'. A gentle, tender girl.
Palometa, Palomita

Pamela Greek 'All sweetness and honey'.
Pam, Pamelina, Pamella, Pammie, Pammy

Pamphila Greek 'All loving'.

Pandora Greek 'Talented, gifted one'.

Pansy Greek 'Fragrant, flower-like'.

Panthea Greek 'Of all the Gods'.
Panthia

Panya Swahili 'Little mouse'.

Paola Italian 'Little'.

Parnella French 'Little rook'.
Parnelle, Pernella, Pernelle

Parthenia Greek 'Sweet virgin'.

Parvaneh Persian 'Butterfly'.

Paschasia Latin 'Born at Easter'.
Parasha

Patience Latin 'Patient one'.
Patienza, Pattie, Patty

Patricia Latin 'Well-born maiden'.
Pat, Patrice, Patrizia, Patsy, Patti, Patty

Paula Latin 'Little'. Feminine of Paul.
Paola, Paule, Paulena, Pauletta, Paulette, Pauli, Paulie, Paulina, Pauline, Paulita, Pavia

Peace Latin 'Tranquillity, calm'.

Pearl Latin 'Precious jewel'.
Pearle, Pearlie, Perl, Perle, Perlie, Perlina, Perline

Pelagia Greek 'Mermaid'.

Penelope Greek 'The weaver'.
Pen, Penny

Peninah Hebrew 'Pearl'.
Peni, Penina

Penthea Greek 'Fifth child'.
Penta, Penthia

Peony Latin 'The gift of healing'.

Perdita Latin 'The lost one'.

Perfecta Spanish 'The most perfect being'.

Perizada Persian 'Born of the fairies'.

Peronel Latin 'A rock'.
Peronelle

Perpetua Latin 'Everlasting'.

Persephone Greek 'Goddess of the underworld'.

Persis Latin 'Woman from Persia'.

Peta Greek 'A rock'.

Petica Latin 'Noble one'.

Petrina Greek 'Steadfast as a rock'. Feminine of Peter.
Perrine, Petra, Petronella, Petronelle, Petronia, Petronilla, Petronille, Petula, Pierette, Pierrette, Pietra

Petula Latin 'Seeker'.

Petunia Indian 'Reddish flower'.

Phedra Greek 'Bright one'.
Phaidra, Phedre

Philadelphia Greek 'Brotherly love'.

Philana Greek 'Friend of humanity'.
Filana

Philantha   Greek 'Lover of flowers'.
Filantha, Philanthe

Philberta   Teutonic 'Very brilliant'.
Filberta, Filberte, Filbertha, Filberthe, Philberthe, Philertha

Philippa   Greek 'Lover of horses'. Feminine of Philip.
Filipa, Filippa, Phillie, Phillipa, Phillippa, Pippa

Phillida   Greek 'Loving woman'.

Philomela   Greek 'Lover of song'.

Philomena   Greek 'Lover of the moon'.

Philothra   Greek 'Pious'.

Phoebe   Greek 'Bright, shining sun'. Feminine of Phoebus (Apollo).
Phebe

Phoenix   Greek 'The eagle'.
Fenix

Photina   Greek 'Light'.

Phyllis   Greek 'A green bough'.
Filida, Filis, Fillida, Fillis, Philis, Phillis, Phylis, Phyllida

Pia   Latin 'Pious'.

Pilar   Spanish 'A foundation or pillar'.

Ping   Chinese 'Duckweed'.

Pinon   Greek 'Pearl'.

Piper   English 'Player of the pipes'.

Placida   Latin 'Peaceful one'.
Placidia

Platona   Greek 'Broad shouldered'. Feminine of Plato.

P
girls

Pomona	Latin 'Fruitful and fertile'.
Poppy	Latin 'Red flower'. *Poppaea*
Portia	Latin 'An offering to God'. *Porcia*
Poupée	French 'Doll'.
Prabha	Hindi 'Light'.
Precious	French 'Precious' or 'dear'.
Preeti	Hindi 'Love'.
Prema	Sanskrit 'Love'. *Prem, Premala*
Prima	Latin 'First born'.
Primalia	Latin 'Like the springtime'.
Primavera	Spanish 'Child of the spring'.
Primrose	Latin 'The first flower of spring'. *Primmie, Primula, Rosa, Rose*
Priscilla	Latin 'Of ancient lineage'. *Pris, Prisca, Prisilla, Prissie*
Proba	Latin 'Honest'.
Prospera	Latin 'Favourable'.
Prudence	Latin 'Cautious foresight'. *Prud, Prudentia, Prudie, Prudy, Prue*
Prunella	French 'Plum coloured'. *Prunelle*
Psyche	Greek 'Of the soul or mind'.

Pulcheria Latin 'Very beautiful'.
Purity Middle English 'Purity'.
Pyrena Greek 'Fiery one'.
Pyrenia
Pythia Greek 'A prophet'.
Pythea

girls

Qadira	Arabic 'Powerful'.	
Qing	Chinese 'Blue'.	
Qiturah	Arabic 'Fragrance'.	
Queena	Teutonic 'The queen'. *Queenie*	
Quenberga	Latin 'Queen's pledge'.	
Quenby	Scandinavian 'Womanly'.	
Quendrida	Latin 'One who threatens the queen'.	
Querida	Spanish 'Beloved one'. *Cherida*	
Questa	French 'Searcher'.	
Quinta	Latin 'The fifth child'. *Quintana, Quintella, Quintilla, Quintina*	
Quintessa	Latin 'Essence'.	
Quisha	African 'Physical and spiritual beauty'.	
Quita	French 'Tranquil'.	

Rabi	Arabic 'The harvest'.
Rabiah	Arabic 'Garden'.
Rachel	Hebrew 'Innocent as a lamb'. *Rachele, Rachelle, Rae, Rahel, Raoghnailt, Raquel, Ray, Shelly*
Rachida	Arabic 'Wise'.
Radella	Anglo-Saxon 'Elf-like adviser'.
Radinka	Slavic 'Alive and joyful'.
Radmilla	Slavic 'Worker for the people'.
Rae	Middle English 'A doe deer'. Also diminutive of Rachel.
Ragini	Sanskrit 'A melody'.
Rahima	Arabic 'Merciful'.
Rainbow	English 'Bow of light'.
Raissa	French 'The believer'. *Raisse*

Rajani   Sanskrit 'Night'.

Ramona   Teutonic 'Wise protector'. Feminine of Raymond.
Mona, Rama, Ramonda, Ramonde

Rana   Sanskrit 'Of royal birth, a queen'.
Ranee, Rani, Rania, Ranique, Rayna

Raphaela   Hebrew 'Blessed healer'.
Rafaela, Rafaella, Raphaella

Rasha   Arabic 'Young gazelle'.

Rashida   African 'Righteous'.

Rashmi   Sanskrit 'Sunlight'.

Raven   English 'Sleek black bird'.

Raymonda   Teutonic 'Wise protector'. Feminine of Raymond.
Raymonde

Rebecca   Hebrew 'The captivator'.
*Beckie, Becky, Bekky, Reba, Rebeca, Rebeka, Rebekah,
Rebekka, Riba*

Rechaba   Hebrew 'Horse woman'.

Regina   Latin 'A queen, born to rule'.
*Gina, Ragan, Raina, Raine, Rayna, Regan, Regine, Reina,
Reine, Rina, Rioghnach*

Rehka   Sanskrit 'Art'.

Reiko   Japanese 'Gratitude'.

Rena   Hebrew 'Song'.
Reena

Renata   Latin 'Born again'.
Renate, Rene, Renee, Rennie

Renee   French 'Born again'.

Renita   Latin 'A rebel'.

Reseda   Latin 'Mignonette flower'.

Reshma   Sanskrit 'Silken'.
Reshmam, Reshmi

Reva   Latin 'Strength regained'.

Rexana   Latin 'Regally graceful'.
Rexanna

Reyhan   Turkish 'Sweet-smelling flower'.

Rhea   Greek 'Mother' or 'Poppy'.
Rea

Rhedyn   Welsh 'Fern'.

Rheta   Greek 'An orator'.

Rhiannon   Welsh 'Nymph'.

Rhianwen   Welsh 'Blessed maiden'.

Rhoda   Greek 'Garland of roses; girl from Rhodes'.
Rhodia, Rodina

Rhodanthe   Greek 'The rose of roses'.

Rhonda   Welsh 'Grand'.

Rhonwen   Welsh 'White lance'.

Ria   Spanish 'The river'.

Ricadonna   Italian 'Ruling lady'.

Ricarda   Teutonic 'Powerful ruler'. Feminine of Richard.
Dickie, Dicky, Richarda, Richarde, Rickie, Ricky

ramia

Riju   Sanskrit 'Innocent'.
Rijuta

Rilla   Teutonic 'A stream or brook'.
Rille, Rillette

Rinah   Hebrew 'Song, joy'.

Risa   Latin 'Laughter'.

Riva   French 'Riverbank'.

Roanna   Latin 'Sweet and gracious'.
Rohanna, Rohanne

Roberta   Anglo-Saxon 'Of shining fame'. Feminine of Robert.
*Bertie, Bobbie, Bobby, Bobette, Bobina, Robertha,
Roberthe, Robinette, Robina, Robinia*

Robia   Teutonic 'Famous'

Robin   Old English 'Bright or shining with fame'.
Robina, Robyn

Rochana   Persian 'Sunrise'.

Rochelle   French 'From the small rock'.
Rochalla, Rochalle, Rochella, Rochette

Roderica   Teutonic 'Famous ruler'. Feminine of Roderick.
Rica, Roddie, Roddy, Rodericka, Rickie

Rohana   Hindu 'Sandalwood, sweet incense'.
Rohane, Rohanna

Rolanda   Teutonic 'From the famed land'. Feminine of Roland.
Orlanda, Orlande, Ro, Rola, Rolande

Romilda   Teutonic 'Glorious warrior maiden'.
Romhilda, Romhilde. Romilde

Romola Latin 'Lady of Rome'.
Roma, Romella, Romelle, Romula

Rona Scandinavian 'Mighty power'.
Rhona, Ronalda

Ronalda Teutonic 'All powerful'. Feminine of Ronald.
Ronalde, Ronnie, Ronny

Rosabel Latin 'Beautiful rose'.
Rosabella, Rosabelle

Rosalind Latin 'Fair and beautiful rose'.
Ros, Rosalinda, Rosaline, Rosalyn, Rosalynd, Roseline, Roselyn, Roslyn, Roz, Rozalind

Rosamond French 'Rose of the world'.
Rosamonda, Rosamund, Rosamunda, Rosemond, Rosemonde, Rosemund, Rosmunda

Rosanna English 'Graceful rose'.
Rosanne

Rosarana Celtic 'Rose bush'.

Rose Greek 'The rose'.
Rasia, Rhodia, Rohesia, Rois, Rosa, Rosalee, Rosaleen, Rosalia, Rosalie, Rosel, Rosella, Rosie

Rosemary Latin 'Dew of the sea'.
Romy, Rosemarie

Rosgrana Celtic 'Sunbeam'.

Rosslyn Welsh 'Moorland lake'.

Rowena Anglo-Saxon 'Friend with white hair'.
Rowenna

Roxana   Persian 'Brilliant dawn'.
Rox, Roxane, Roxanna, Roxanne, Roxie, Roxina, Roxine, Roxy

Royale   French 'Regal being'. Feminine of Roy.

Rozene   Native American 'Rose'.

Ruby   Latin 'Precious red jewel'.
Rubetta, Rubette, Rubia, Rubie, Rubina

Rucita   Sanskrit 'Shining'.

Rudelle   Teutonic 'Famous person'.
Rudella

Rufina   Latin 'Red-haired one'.

Rugina   Latin 'Girl with bright red hair'.

Rula   Latin 'A sovereign'.

Rupak   Sanskrit 'Beautiful'.
Rupali, Rupashi, Rupashri

Ruri   Japanese 'Emerald'.

Ruth   Hebrew 'Compassionate and beautiful'.
Ruthie

Rutilia   Latin 'Fiery red'.

S

Saba   Greek 'Woman of Sheba'.
Sheba

Sabella   Latin 'The wise'.
Sabelle

Sabina   Latin 'Woman of Sabine'.
Bina, Binnie, Sabine, Saidhbhain, Savina

Sabira   Arabic 'Patient'.

Sabra   Hebrew 'The restful one'.

Sabrina   Latin 'A princess'.
Brina, Sabrine

Sacha   Greek 'Helpmate'.
Sasha

Sacharissa   Greek 'Sweet'.

Sadira   Persian 'The lotus eater'.

Saffron   English From the plant.

Safia   Arabic 'Pure'.

Sahlah   Arabic 'Smooth'.

Sai   Japanese 'Intelligence'.

Sajala   Sanskrit 'Clouds'.
Sajal

Sakhi   Sanskrit 'Friend'.
Sakina

Salema   Hebrew 'Girl of peace'.
Selemas, Selima

Saliha   Arabic 'Goodness'.

Salima   Arabic 'Safe' or 'Unharmed'.

Salina   Greek 'From the salty place'.

Salome   Hebrew 'Peace'.
Saloma, Salomi

Salvia   Latin 'Sage herb'.
Salvina

Samala   Hebrew 'Asked of God'.

Samantha   Aramaic 'A listener'.

Samara   Hebrew 'Watchful, cautious, guarded by God'.

Samira   Arabic 'Entertaining'.

Samuela   Hebrew 'His name is God'. Feminine of Samuel.
Samella, Samelle, Samuella, Samuelle

Sancia   Latin 'Sacred'.
Sancha, Sanchia

Sandip   Sanskrit 'Beautiful one.'

Sanjay Sanskrit 'Charioteer'.

Sapphira Greek 'Eyes of sapphire colour'.
Sapphire

Sarah Hebrew 'Princess'.
Morag, Sadella, Sadie, Sadye, Sal, Salaidh, Sallie, Sally, Sara, Sarene, Sarette, Sari, Sarine, Sharie, Zara

Saree Arabic 'Most noble'.

Savanna Spanish 'An open plain'.

Saxona Teutonic 'A sword bearer'.

Scarlett Middle English 'Scarlet coloured'.
Scarlet, Scarletta

Scholastica Latin 'Scholar'.

Sebastiane Latin 'Revered one'.
Sebastianan, Sebastianna, Sebastianne, Sebastienna, Sebastienne

Sebila Latin 'Wise old woman'.

Secunda Latin 'Second born'.

Seema Hebrew 'Treasure'.

Seiran Welsh 'Sparkling'.

Seirol Welsh 'Light'.

Selam Sudanese 'Peaceful'.

Selena Greek 'The Moon'.
Celene, Celie, Celina, Celinda, Salene, Sela, Selene, Selia, Selie, Selina, Selinda, Sena, Lena

Selma Celtic 'The fair'. Also derivative of Anselma.

Semele Latin 'The single one'.
Semelia

Semira   Hebrew 'Height of the heavens'.

Senalda   Spanish 'A sign'.

Septima   Latin 'Seventh born'.

Seraphina   Hebrew 'The ardent believer, one with a burning faith'.
Sera, Serafina, Serafine, Seraphine

Serena   Latin 'Bright tranquil one'.

Serilda   Teutonic 'Armoured battle maid'.
Serhilda, Serhilde, Serilde

Shafira   Arabic 'Eminent, honourable'.

Shannon   Gaelic 'Small but wise'.
Shannah

Sharon   Hebrew 'A princess of exotic beauty'.
Shari, Sharri, Sharron, Sharry, Sherry

Sheena   Gaelic 'Dim-sighted'.
Sheela, Sheelah, Sheilah

Sheila   Celtic 'Musical'. Variation of Cecilia.
Selia, Sheela, Shelagh, Sheelah, Sheilah

Shelah   Hebrew 'Asked for'.
Shava, Shea, Shela, Sheva, Sheya

Shelby   Old English 'From the estate'.

Shelley   English 'From the edge of the meadow'.

Shereen   Arabic 'Sweet'.

Shifra   Hebrew 'Beautiful'.

Shina   Japanese 'Good virtue'.

Shiri   Hebrew 'My song'.

Shirley Anglo-Saxon 'From the white meadow'.
Sheri, Sherry, Sheryl, Shirlee, Shirleen, Shirlene, Shirlie

Shoshana Hebrew 'Rose'.

Shula Arabic 'Flame, brightness'.

Shulamith Hebrew 'Peace'.

Sida Greek 'Water lily'.

Sidra Latin 'Glittering lady of the stars'.
Sidria

Sierna Greek 'A sweetly singing mermaid'.

Sierra Irish 'Black'.

Sigfreda Teutonic 'Victorious and peaceful'.
Sigfrieda, Sigfriede

Signa Latin 'Signed on the heart'.

Sigrid Norse 'Victorious counsellor'.
Sigrath, Sigrud, Sigurd

Silvana Latin 'Wood dweller'.

Simone Hebrew 'Heard by the Lord'. Feminine of Simon/Simeon.
Simona, Simonetta, Simonette

Sinead Gaelic 'God's gift of grace'. A form of Jane.

Siobhan Gaelic 'Gift of God'. Variation of Jane.

Sirena Greek 'Sweet singing mermaid'.
Sireen, Sirene

Skylar Dutch 'Sheltering'.
Skye

Smita Sanskrit 'Smiling'.

Snowdrop	English From the plant.
Solah	Latin 'Alone'. *Solita*
Solana	Spanish 'Sunshine'.
Solange	Latin 'Good shepherdess'.
Solita	Latin 'Solitary one'.
Solvig	Teutonic 'Victorious battle maid'.
Sophia	Greek 'Wisdom'. *Beathag, Sadhbh, Sadhbha, Sofia, Sofie, Sonia, Sonja, Sonya, Sophie, Sophy*
Sophie	Popular variation of Sophia.
Sophronia	Greek 'Sensible one'.
Sorcha	Gaelic 'Bright one'.
Sparkle	Dutch 'Gleaming'.
Sperata	Latin 'Hoped for'.
Spring	English 'Joyous season'.
Starr	English 'A star'. *Star*
Stephanie	Greek 'A crown, garland'. Feminine of Stephen. *Stefa, Steffie, Stepha, Stephania, Stephena, Stephenia, Stephenie, Stevana, Stevania, Stevie*
Storm	Anglo-Saxon 'A tempest'.
Sucheta	Sanskrit 'With a beautiful mind'. *Suchi, Suchira, Suchita, Suchitra*
Sulia	Latin 'Downy, youthful'.
Sulwyn	Welsh 'Beautiful as the sun'.

Sumalee Thai 'Beautiful flower'.

Sumi Japanese 'Refined'.

Sunita Hindi 'Good conduct and deeds'.

Sunny Anglo-Saxon 'Bright and cheerful'.

Supriya Sanskrit 'Loved'.
Supriti

Susan Hebrew 'Graceful lily'.
*Sue, Sukey, Suki, Suky, Susana, Susanna, Susannah,
Susanne, Susette, Susi, Susie, Susy, Suzanna, Suzanne,
Suzette, Suzie, Zsa, Zsa-Zsa*

Sushila Sanskrit 'Well behaved'.

Svetlana German 'A star'.

Sybil Greek 'Prophetess'.
*Cybil, Sib, Sibbie, Sibby, Sibel, Sibell, Sibella, Sibie, Sibil,
Sibilla, Sibille, Sibyl*

Sydel Hebrew 'That enchantress'.
Sydelle

Sydney Hebrew 'The enticer'.
Sid, Sidney, Sidonia, Sidonie, Syd

Sylgwyn Welsh 'Born on Whit Sunday'.

Sylvana Latin 'From the woods'.

Sylvia Latin 'From the forest'.
*Sil, Silva, Silvana, Silvia, Silvie, Slyvana, Syl, Sylva, Zilva,
Zilvia*

Syna Greek 'Together'.
Syne

Syntyche Greek 'With good fortune'.

girls

Tabina	Arabic 'Muhammed's follower'.
Tabitha	Aramaic 'The gazelle'. *Tabbie, Tabby, Tabithe*
Tacitah	Latin 'Silence'. *Tacita*
Tacy	Latin 'Peace'.
Tahani	Arabic 'Congratulations'.
Tahira	Arabic 'Pure'.
Takara	Japanese/Sanskrit 'Treasure' (Japanese) or 'star' (Sanskrit).
Talia	Greek 'Blooming'.
Taliba	Arabic 'Student'.
Talitha	Aramaic 'The maiden'.
Tallulah	Native American 'Laughing water'. *Tallie, Tallu, Tallula, Tally*

Tama Japanese 'Jewel'.

Tamali Sanskrit 'Tree with the black bark'.
Tamalika

Tamara Hebrew 'Palm tree'.
Tamar, Tammie, Tammy

Tammy Hebrew 'Perfection'. Also diminutive of Tamara.

Tangerine Anglo-Saxon 'Girl from Tangiers'.

Tangwystl Welsh 'Peace pledge'.

Tani Japanese 'Valley'.

Tania Russian 'The fairy queen'. Also diminutive of Titania.
Tanya

Tansy Latin 'Tenacious'.
Tandi

Tanuka Sanskrit 'Slender'.

Tara Gaelic 'Towering rock'.
Tarah

Tate Old English 'To be cheerful'.
Tatum

Tatiana Latin 'Silver-haired one'.

Taylor Middle English 'A tailor'.

Tegan Welsh 'Beautiful'.

Tegwen Welsh 'Beautiful and blessed'.

Temira Hebrew 'Tall'.
Timora

Tempest French 'Stormy one'.
Tempesta, Tempeste

Terentia Greek 'Guardian'. Feminine of Terence.
Terencia, Teri, Terri, Terrie, Terry

Teresa Greek 'The harvester'.
Terese, Teresina, Teresita, Teressa, Terri, Terrie, Terry, Tess, Tessa, Tessie, Tessy, Theresa, Therese, Tracie, Tracy, Zita

Tertia Latin 'Third child'.

Terza Greek 'Girl from the farm'.

Tessa Greek 'Fourth child'. Also variation of Teresa.

Tewdews Welsh 'Divinely given'.

Thaddea Greek 'Courageous being'.
Thada, Thadda

Thalassa Greek 'From the sea'.

Thalia Greek 'Luxurious blossom'.

Thea Greek 'Goddess'. Also diminutive of Dorothea, Theadora, Anthea, etc.

Theano Greek 'Divine name'.
Theana

Thecla Greek 'Divine follower'.
Tecla, Thekla

Thelma Greek 'The nursling'.

Theodora Greek 'Gift of God'. Another version of Dorothy.
Dora, Feadora, Feadore, Fedora, Fedore, Feodora, Feodore, Teddie, Teodora, Thea, Theadora, Theo and all forms of Dorothy

Theola Greek 'Sent from God'.
Theo, Lola

Theone Greek 'In the name of God'.
Theona

Theophania Greek 'Beloved of God'.
Theofila, Theofilia, Theophilia

Theophila Greek 'Appearance of God'.
*Theafania, Theofanie, Theaphania, Theophanie, Tiffanie,
Tiffy*

Theora Greek 'Watcher for God'.

Thera Greek 'Wild, untamed one'.

Thetis Greek 'Positive one'.
Thetys

Thirza Hebrew 'Pleasantness'.
Thyrza, Tirza

Thomasina Hebrew 'The twin'. Feminine of Thomas.
*Tamsin, Thomasa, Thomase, Thomasine, Tomasa,
Tomase, Tomasina, Tomasine*

Thora Norse 'Thunder'.

Thorberta Norse 'Brilliance of Thor'.
Thorberte, Thorbertha, Thorberthe

Thordis Norse 'Spirit of Thor'.
Thordia, Thordie

Thyra Greek 'Shield bearer'.

Tiara Latin 'Crowned'.

Tibelda Teutonic 'Boldest person'.

Tiberia Latin 'From the Tiber'.

Tiffany Hebrew 'Three, the trinity'.

Timothea Greek 'Honouring God'.
Tim, Timmie, Timmy

Tirza Spanish 'Cypress'.

Tita Latin 'Honoured title'.

Titania Greek 'Giantess'. Also the name of the queen of fairies.
Tania, Tanya

Tizane Hungarian 'A gypsy'.

Tobey Hebrew 'God is good'.
Tobe, Tobi, Toby

Toni Japanese 'Riches'.

Topaz Latin 'The topaz gem'.

Tracy Gaelic 'Battler'. Also derivative of Teresa.
Tracey

Traviata Italian 'The frail one'.

Triantafilia Greek 'Rose'.

Trilby Italian 'A singer who trills'.

Trina Greek 'Girl of purity'.

Trista Latin 'Melancholia, sorrow'.

Trudy Teutonic 'Loved one'. Also diminutive of Gertrude.
Trudey, Trudi, Trudie

Tryphena Latin 'The delicate one'.
Triphena, Triphenia, Tryphenia

Tuesday Anglo-Saxon 'Born on Tuesday'.

Tullia Gaelic 'Peaceful one'.

Turaya Arabic 'Star'.

Twyla Middle English 'Woven of double thread'.

Tyne Old English 'River'.

Tyra Scandinavian 'Battler'.

Uda Teutonic 'Prosperous'. A child of fortune.
Udella, Udelle

Ula Teutonic/Celtic 'The inheritor' (Teutonic) or 'jewel of the sea' (Celtic).
Oola

Ulima Arabic 'The learned one'.

Ulrica Teutonic 'Ruler of all'.
Elrica, Rica, Ulrika

Ultima Latin 'The most distant'.

Ulva Teutonic 'The she-wolf'. A symbol of bravery.

Umar Arabic 'Flourishing'.

Umeko Japanese 'Plum-blossom child'.

Una Latin 'One'. The one and only girl.
Ona, Oona, Oonagh

Unity Middle English 'Unity'.

Urania Greek 'Heavenly'.

Urbana Latin 'Born in the town'.

Urith Old German 'Deserving'.

Ursula Latin 'The she-bear'.
Ora, Orsa, Orsola, Ursa, Ursel, Ursie, Ursola, Ursule, Ursulette, Ursuline, Ursy

Usha Sanskrit 'Dawn'.

Ushakiran Sanskrit 'The first rays of the sun'.

Ushashi Sanskrit 'Morning'

Uta German 'Rich'.

Utina Native American 'Woman from my country'.

Utsa Sanskrit 'Spring'.

Vahsti   Persian 'Beautiful one'.

Vala   Teutonic 'The chosen one'.

Valborga   Teutonic 'Protecting ruler'.
Valburga, Walborga, Walburga

Valda   Teutonic 'Ruler'.
Walda, Welda

Valentina   Latin 'Strong and vigorous'.
Val, Valeda, Valencia, Valentia, Valentine, Valera, Valida, Vallie

Valerie   French 'Strong'.
Val, Valeria, Valery, Vallie, Valora, Valorey, Valorie, Valory

Valeska   Slavic 'Glorious ruler'.
Waleska

Valma   Welsh 'Mayflower'.
Valmai

Valonia   Latin 'From the vale'.
Valona

Vanda   Teutonic 'Family'.

Vanessa   Greek 'The butterfly'.
Van, Vania, Vanna, Vanni, Vannie, Vanny, Vanya

Vania   Hebrew 'God's precious gift'.
Vanina

Vanita   Sanskrit 'Desired'.

Varina   Slavic 'Stranger'.

Vashti   Persian 'The most beautiful'.

Veda   Sanskrit 'Wisdom and knowledge'.
Vedis

Vedette   Italian 'The sentinel'.
Vedetta

Vega   Arabic 'The great one'.

Velda   Teutonic 'Very wise'.
Valida

Velika   Slavic 'The falling one'.
Velica

Velvet   English 'Soft as velvet'.

Venetia   Latin 'Lady of Venice'.

Ventura   Spanish 'Happiness and good luck'.

Venus   Latin 'Loveliness, beauty'.
Venita, Vinita, Vinnie, Vinny

Vera   Latin 'Truth'.
Vere, Verena, Verene, Veria, Verina, Verine

Verbena Latin 'The sacred bough'.

Verda Latin 'Fresh youth'.

Verity Latin 'Truth'.

Verna Latin 'Spring-like'.
Verda, Verena, Verneta, Vernice, Vernis, Vernita, Virina, Virna

Verona Latin 'Lady of Verona'.

Veronica Latin 'True image'. Also variation of Bernice.
Ronnie, Ronny, Veronique, Vonnie, Vony, and all variations of Bernice

Vesna Slavic 'Spring'.

Vespera Latin 'The evening star'.

Vesta Latin 'Guardian of the sacred flame'.

Vevila Gaelic 'Melodious one'.

Victoria Latin 'The victorious one'.
Tory, Vicki, Vicky, Victorine, Victorie, Vitoria, Vittoria

Vida Hebrew 'Beloved one'. Feminine of David.

Vidette Hebrew 'Beloved'.

Vidonia Portuguese 'Vine branch'.

Vidula Sanskrit 'The moon'.

Vigilia Latin 'The alert, vigilant'.

Vignette French 'The little vine'.

Vijaya Sanskrit 'Victory'.

Villette French 'From the village'.

Vina Spanish 'From the vineyard'.

Vinaya   Sanskrit 'Modest'.

Vincentia   Latin 'The conqueror'. Feminine of Vincent.
Vicenta, Vincencia

Violet   Latin 'Modest flower'.
Vi, Viola, Violante, Violetta, Violette, Yolanda, Yolande, Yolanthe

Virdis   Latin 'Fresh, blooming'.

Virgilia   Latin 'The staff bearer'.

Virginia   Latin 'The virgin, maidenly and pure'.
Ginger, Ginnie, Ginny, Jinny, Virgi, Virgie, Virginie, Virgy

Viridis   Latin 'The green bough'.

Vita   Latin 'Life'. One who likes living.
Evita, Veta, Vitia

Viveca   Latin/Scandinavian 'Living voice'.

Vivian   Latin 'Alive'. Vivid and vibrant with life.
Viv, Vivi, Vivia, Viviana, Viviane, Vivie, Vivien, Viviene, Vivienna, Vivienne, Vivyan, Vyvyan

Volante   Latin 'The flying one'.

Voleta   French 'A floating veil'.
Voletta

girls

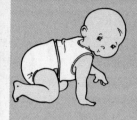

Wahilda   Arabic 'Unique'.

Wahkuna   Native American 'Beautiful'.

Walida   Arabic 'New-born girl'.

Wallis   Anglo-Saxon 'The Welshwoman, the stranger'.
Wallace, Wallie, Wally

Wanda   Teutonic 'The wanderer'.
Wandie, Wandis, Wenda, Wendeline

Wanetta   Anglo-Saxon 'The pale one'.
Wanette

Warda   Teutonic 'The guardian'.

Wasima   Arabic 'Pretty'.

Wendy   English Created by J.M. Barrie for *Peter Pan*.

Whitney   Old English 'From the white island'.

Wilfreda   Teutonic 'The peacemaker'. Feminine of Wilfred.
Freda, Freddie, Wilf, Wilfreida, Wilfrieda

Wilhelmina Teutonic 'The protectress'.
Billie, Billy, Guilla, Helma, Mina, Minnie, Minny, Velma, Welma, Willa, Willie, Willy, Wilma

Willa Anglo-Saxon 'Desirable'. Also diminutive of Wilhelmina.

Willow English Plant name.

Wilona Old English 'Desired'.

Winema Native American 'Chief of the tribe'.

Winifred Teutonic 'Peaceful friend'. Feminine of Winfred.
Winifreida, Winifrida, Winifrieda, Winnie, Winny, Wynn

Winna African 'Friend'.
Winnah

Winola Teutonic 'Gracious friend'.

Winona American-Indian 'First born daughter'.
Wenona, Wenonah, Winonah

Winsome English 'Pleasant, attractive'.

Wren Old English 'Wren'.

Wyanet Native American 'Very beautiful'.

Wylda Teutonic 'Rebellious'.

Wylma Teutonic 'Resolute'.

Wynne Celtic 'Fair, white maiden'.
Win, Wyne

girls

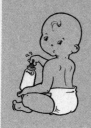

Xanthe	Greek 'Golden blonde'.
Xanthippe	Greek The wife of Socrates.
Xaverie	Aramaic 'Bright'.
Xaviera	Spanish 'Owner of the home'.
Xena	Greek 'Hospitality'. *Xene, Xenia, Zenia*
Xiaoli	Chinese 'Small and beautiful'.
Xiiaoying	Chinese 'Small flower'.
Ximena	Greek 'Heroine'.
Xylia	Greek 'From the woods'. *Xyline, Xylona*

Yaffa	Hebrew 'Beautiful',
Yakira	Hebrew 'Valuable'.
Yasmeen	Persian 'Flower'.
Yasu	Japanese 'Tranquil'.
Yedda	Anglo-Saxon 'One with a melodious voice'.
Yeira	Hebrew 'Light'.
Yepa	Native American 'Snow girl'.
Yesima	Hebrew 'Right hand, strength'.
Yetta	Anglo-Saxon 'To give, the giver'. Also diminutive of Henrietta.
Yona	Korean 'Lotus blossom'.
Yoshe	Japanese 'Beautiful'.
Yoshiko	Japanese 'Good'.
Yovela	Hebrew 'Rejoicing'.
Yvonne	French 'Archer with the yew bow'. *Evette, Evonne, Ivonne, Von, Vonnie, Yevetta, Yevette, Yvetta, Yvette, Yvona*

Z

Zabrina Anglo-Saxon 'Noble maiden'.

Zada Arabic 'Lucky one'. Fortune's favourite.

Zahra Arabic 'Blossom'.

Zakira Arabic 'Remembrance'.

Zamira Hebrew 'Song'.

Zana Persian 'Woman'.

Zara Hebrew 'Brightness of dawn'. Also derivative of Sarah.
Zarah, Zaria

Zarifa Arabic 'Graceful',

Zea Latin 'Ripened grain'.

Zebada Hebrew 'Gift of the Lord'.

Zelia Greek 'Devoted to duty'.
Zele, Zelie, Zelina

Zella Hebrew 'Shadow'.

Zelosa Greek 'Jealous one'.

Zena Greek 'The hospitable one'.

Zenobia Greek 'Zeus gave life'.
Zena, Zenaida, Zenda, Zenia, Zenina, Zenna, Zennie, Zenorbie

Zenobia Arabic 'Ornament to her father'.

Zephirah Hebrew 'Dawn'.

Zera Hebrew 'Seeds'.

Zerelda Old German 'Armoured warrior maid'.

Zerlina Teutonic 'Serene beauty'.
Zerla, Zerline

Zerlinda Hebrew 'Beautiful as the dawn'.

Zetta Anglo-Saxon 'Sixth born'.
Zita, Zitao

Zeva Greek 'Sword'.

Zia Sanskrit 'Enlightened'.

Zian Hebrew 'Abundance'.
Zena, Zinah

Zila Sanskrit 'A shady place'.

Zilla Hebrew 'Shadow'.
Zillah

Zilpah Hebrew 'Dropping'.

Zinnia Latin 'The zinnia flower'.
Zinia

Zippora Hebrew 'Trumpet' or 'Sparrow'.
Zipporah

Ziva	Hebrew 'Brightness'.
Zoë	Greek 'Life'.
Zofeyah	Hebrew 'God sees'.
Zohara	Hebrew 'The bright child'.
Zona	Latin 'A girdle'. The belt of Orion. *Zonie*
Zora	Latin 'The dawn'. *Zorah, Zorana, Zorina, Zorine*
Zosima	Greek 'Wealthy woman'.
Zuleika	Arabic 'Fair'.
Zulema	Arabic/Hebrew 'Peace'.

Boys

boys

Aaron Hebrew 'Exalted'. Brother of Moses.
Aron, Haroun

Abba Hebrew 'Father'.

Abbott Anglo-Saxon 'Father of the abbey'.
Abbe, Abbot, Abott

Abdi Hebrew 'My servant'.

Abdiel Hebrew 'Servant of God'.

Abdon Hebrew 'Son of'.

Abdul Arabic 'Son of'.
Abdel

Abdullah Arabic 'Servant of Allah'.

Abel Hebrew 'Breath'. The first murder victim recorded, according to the Bible.

Abelard Teutonic 'Nobly resolute'.

Abir Hebrew 'Strong'.
Abiri

Abisha Hebrew 'God's gift'.

Abner Hebrew 'Father of light'.

Abraham Hebrew 'Father of multitudes'. The original patriarch.
Abe, Abie, Abram, Abran, Avram, Bram, Ibrahim

Absalom Hebrew 'Father of peace'.
Absolom

Ace Latin 'Unity'.
Acey

Achilles Greek 'Swift'.

Ackerley Anglo-Saxon 'From the acre meadow'.

Ackley Anglo-Saxon/Teutonic 'From the oak tree meadow'.

Acton Old English 'Town near oak trees'.

Adair Gaelic 'From the oak tree near the ford'.

Adalard Teutonic 'Noble and brave'.
Adelard, Adhelard

Adalric Old German 'Noble ruler'.
Adelric

Adam Hebrew 'Of the red earth'. The first man, according to the Bible.

Adamo, Adan, Adao, Adhamh

Adar Hebrew 'Fiery'.

Addison Anglo-Saxon 'Adam's son'.

Addy Teutonic 'Awesome, noble'.

Ademar Teutonic 'Fierce, noble, famous'.
Ademaro

Adesh   Sanskrit 'Command'.

Adham   Arabic 'Black'.

Adhar   Arabic 'Waiting'.

Adin   Hebrew 'Sensual'.
           Adan

Adlai   Hebrew 'My witness, my ornament'.

Adler   Teutonic 'Eagle'. One of keen perception.

Adley   Hebrew 'Fair-minded'.

Adney   Anglo-Saxon 'One who lives on the island'.

Adolph   Teutonic 'Noble wolf'.
           *Ad, Adolf, Adolfus, Adolphe, Adolpho, Adolphus, Dolf,
           Dolph*

Adon   Hebrew 'Lord'. The sacred Hebrew word for God.

Adrian   Latin 'Dark one' or 'man from the sea'.
           Ade, Adriano, Adrien, Hadrian

Aeneas   Greek 'The much-praised one'. The defender of Troy.
           Eneas

Afdal   Arabic 'Excellent'.

Afif   Arabic 'Virtuous'.

Agamemnon Greek 'Resolute'.

Agilard   Teutonic 'Formidably bright'.

Ahern   Gaelic 'Horse lord' or 'horse owner'.
           Ahearn, Aherin, Aherne, Hearn, Hearne

Ahmed   Arabic 'Most highly praised'.

Ahren   Teutonic 'The eagle'.

Aidan Gaelic 'Little fiery one'.
Adan, Eden

Aiken Anglo-Saxon 'Little Adam'.
Aickin, Aokin

Aimery Teutonic 'Industrious ruler'.

Aimon French from Teutonic 'House'.

Ainsley Anglo-Saxon 'Meadow of the respected one'.

Ajax Greek 'Eagle'.

Ajay Sanskrit 'Invincible'.

Akbar Arabic 'Great'.

Akmal Arabic 'Perfect'.

Akram Arabic 'Noble, generous'.

Aladdin Arabic 'Servant of Allah'.

Alair Gaelic 'Cheerful'.

Alam Arabic/Sanskrit 'Universe'.
Alaam

Alan Gaelic 'Cheerful harmony'.
Ailean, Ailin, Alain, Aland, Alano, Alanson, Allan, Allen, Allyn

Alard German 'Noble ruler'.

Alaric Teutonic 'Ruler of all'.
Alarick, Rich, Richie, Rick, Rickie, Ricky, Ricy, Ulric, Ulrich, Ulrick

Alban Latin 'White complexion'. A man of outstandingly fair colouring.
Albin, Aleb, Alva, Aubin

Albern Anglo-Saxon 'Noble warrior'.

Albert   Teutonic 'Noble and illustrious'.

Adelbert, Ailbert, Aldabert, Aubert, Bert, Berty, Delbert, Elbert

Alcander   Greek 'Strong'.

Alcott   Anglo-Saxon 'One who lives at the old cottage'.

Alden   Anglo-Saxon 'Wise old friend'. One on whom friends can rely.

Aldin, Aldwin, Aldwyn, Elden, Eldin

Alder   Anglo-Saxon 'At the alder tree'.

Aldis   Anglo-Saxon 'From the old house'.
Aldous, Aldus

Aldo   Teutonic 'Old, wise and rich'.

Aldrich   Anglo-Saxon 'Wise old ruler'.
Aldric, Aldridge, Alric, Eldric, Eldrich

Aled   Welsh Name of a Welsh river.

Aleem   Sanskrit 'Knowledgeable'.

Alem   Arabic 'Wise man'.

Aleron   Latin 'The eagle'.

Alex   Popular variation of Alexander.

Alexander   Greek 'Helper and protector of mankind'.
Alasdair, Alastair, Alasteir, Alaster, Alec, Aleck, Alejandro, Alejo, Aleksandr, Alessandro, Alex, Alexis, Alick, Alister, Allister, Alsandair, Sander, Sandie, Sandy, Sasha, Saunders

Alfie   Popular variation of Alfred.

Alfred   Anglo-Saxon 'The wise counsel of the elf'.
Aelfred, Ailfrid, Al, Alf, Alfie, Alfredo, Alfy

Algernon French 'The whiskered one'. The man with a moustache or beard.

Al, Algie, Algy

Algis French from Teutonic 'Spear'.

Ali Sanskrit/Arabic 'Protected by god' (Sanskrit) or 'greatest, noble, sublime' (Arabic).

Alim Arabic 'Scholar'.

Alison Anglo-Saxon 'Son of a nobleman' or 'Alice's son'.
Al, Allie, Allison

Allard Anglo-Saxon 'Noble and brave'.
Aethelard, Aethelhard, Alard, Ethelard

Almund Teutonic 'Protection'.

Aloysius Latin 'Famous warrior'.
Alabhaois, Aloys, Lewis, Louis, Ludwig

Alpin Early Scottish 'Blond one'. Name borne by the descendants of the earliest Scottish clan McAlpin.

Alston Anglo-Saxon 'From the old village'.

Altman Teutonic 'Old, wise man'.

Alton Anglo-Saxon 'One who lives in the old town'.

Alvah Hebrew 'The exalted one'.
Alvar

Alvin Teutonic 'Friend of all' or 'noble friend'.
Aldwin, Aloin, Aluin, Aluino, Alvan, Alwin, Alwyn

Amadeo Spanish 'Beloved of God'.

Amadour French from Latin 'Lovable'.
Amadeus

Amasa Hebrew 'Burden bearer'.

Ambert Teutonic 'Shining, bright light'.

Ambrose Latin 'Belonging to the divine immortals'.
Ambroise, Ambros, Ambrosi, Ambrosio, Ambrosius, Amby, Brose, Emrys, Gino

Amijad Arabic 'Glorious'.

Amil Arabic/Sanskrit 'Industrious, invaluable'.

Amin Arabic/Hebrew/Sanskrit 'Trustworthy, honest' (Arabic/Hebrew) or 'divine grace' (Sanskrit).
Ameen

Amirov Hebrew 'My people are great'.

Amitan Hebrew 'True, faithful'.

Ammon Egyptian 'The hidden'.

Amos Hebrew 'A burden'. One used to tackling difficult problems.

Amram Arabic 'Life'.

Amrit Sanskrit 'Water of life'.

Anatole Greek 'From the East'.
Anatol, Anatolio

Ancel German 'God-like'.
Ancell

Andrew Greek 'Strong and manly'. The patron saint of Scotland.
Aindreas, Anders, Anderson, Andie, Andonis, Andre, Andreas, Andrej, Andrien, Andris, Andy, Drew

Aneurin Celtic 'Truly golden'.
Nye

Angelo Italian 'Saintly messenger'.
Ange, Angell

A
boys

Angus Celtic 'Outstanding and exceptional man'. One of unparalleled strength.

Angwyn Welsh 'Very handsome'.

Annan Celtic 'From the stream'.

Anniss Arabic 'Charming'.

Ansel French 'Nobleman's follower'.
Ansell

Anselm Teutonic 'Divine helmet'.
Anse, Ansel, Anselme, Anshelm

Ansley Anglo-Saxon 'From Ann's meadow'.

Anson Anglo-Saxon 'Ann's son'.

Anstice Greek 'The resurrected'. One who returns to life after death.
Anstiss

Anthony Latin 'Of inestimable worth'. A man without peer.
Anntoin, Antin, Antoine, Anton, Antonino, Antonio, Antons, Antony, Tony

Anwell Celtic 'Beloved one'.
Anwyl, Anwyll

Anyon Celtic 'The anvil'. One on whom all the finest characteristics have been forged.

Archard Teutonic 'Sacred and powerful'.
Archerd

Archer Anglo-Saxon 'The bowman'.

Archibald Teutonic 'Noble and truly bold'. A brave and sacred warrior.
Arch, Archaimbaud, Archambault, Archer, Archibaldo, Archie, Archimbald, Archy, Arkady, Gilleasbuig

Archie Popular variation of Archibald.

Arden Latin 'Ardent, fiery, fervent, sincere'. Intensely loyal.
Ardin

Ardley Anglo-Saxon 'From the domestic meadow'.

Arel Hebrew 'Lion of God'.

Aretino Greek 'Victorious'.

Argus Greek 'The watchful one'. The giant with one hundred eyes, who saw everything at once.

Argyle Gaelic 'From the land of the Gaels'.

Aric Anglo-Saxon 'Sacred ruler'.
Rick, Rickie, Ricky

Ariel Hebrew 'Lion of God'.

Arlen Gaelic 'Pledge'.
Airleas, Arlin

Arlie Anglo-Saxon 'From the rabbit meadow'.
Arley, Arly, Harley, Harly

Armand Teutonic 'Man of the army'. The military man personified.
Armando, Armin, Armond

Armstrong Anglo-Saxon 'Strong arm'. The tough warrior who could wield a battle axe.

Arnall Teutonic 'Gracious eagle'. The nobleman who is also a gentleman.

Arnett French 'Little eagle'.
Arnatt, Arnott

Arney Teutonic 'The eagle'.
Arne, Arnie

Arnold Teutonic 'Strong as an eagle'
Arnald, Arnaldo, Arnaud, Arne, Arnie, Arno

Artemis   Greek 'Gift of Artemis'.
Artemas

Arthur   Celtic 'The noble bear man' or 'Strong as a rock'. The semi-legendary King of Britain, who founded the Round Table.
Art, Artair, Artie, Artur, Arturo, Artus, Aurthur

Arundel   Anglo-Saxon 'One who lives with eagles'. Man who shares their keen sight.

Arvad   Hebrew 'The wanderer'.
Arpad

Arval   Latin 'Much lamented'.
Arvel

Arvin   Teutonic 'Friend of the people'. The first true socialist.

Asa   Hebrew 'The healer'.

Ascelin   German 'Of the moon'.
Aceline

Ascot   Anglo-Saxon 'Owner of the east cottage'.
Ascott

Ashburn   Anglo-Saxon 'The brook by the ash tree'.

Ashby   Anglo-Saxon 'Ash tree farm'.
Ashbey, Ashton

Asher   Hebrew 'The laughing one'.

Ashford   Anglo-Saxon 'One who lives in the ford by the ash tree'.

Ashim   Sanskrit 'Without limit'.
Aseem

Ashley   Anglo-Saxon 'One who lives in the ash tree meadow'.

Ashlin   Anglo-Saxon 'One who lives by the ash tree pool'.

Ashraf   Arabic 'More noble' or 'more honourable'.

Ashton   Anglo-Saxon 'One who lives at the ash tree farm'.

Ashwani   Hindi 'First of 27 galaxies revolving round the moon'.

Aslam   Sanskrit/Arabic 'Greeting' (Sanskrit) or 'safe' (Arabic).

Astrophel   Greek 'Star lover'.

Atherton   Anglo-Saxon 'One who lives at the spring farm'.

Atley   Anglo-Saxon 'One who lives in the meadow'.

Atwater   Anglo-Saxon 'One who lives by the water'.

Atwell   Anglo-Saxon 'From the spring'. One who built his home by a natural well.

Atwood   Anglo-Saxon 'From the forest'.
Attwood, Atwoode

Auberon   Teutonic 'Noble'.
Oberon

Aubrey   Teutonic 'Elf ruler'. The golden-haired king of the spirit world.
Alberik, Aube, Auberon

Audley   Old English 'Prospering'.

August   Latin 'Exalted one'.
Agosto, Agustin, Augie, Auguste, Augustin, Augustine, Augustus, Austen, Austin, Gus, Gussy

Auryn   Welsh 'Gold'.

Avan   Hebrew 'Proud'.
Evan

Averill   Anglo-Saxon 'Boar-like' or 'born in April'.
Averel, Averell, Averil, Everild

Avery   Anglo-Saxon 'Ruler of the elves'.

Aviv   Hebrew 'Spring'.

Axel   Teutonic 'Father of peace'.

Axton   Anglo-Saxon 'Stone of the sword fighter'. The whetstone of the warrior's sword.

Aylmer   Anglo-Saxon 'Noble and famous'.

Aylward   Anglo-Saxon 'Awe-inspiring guardian'.

Aylwin   Teutonic 'Devoted friend'.

Aymon   Old French 'Home'

Ayward   Old English 'Noble guardian'.

Azarias   Hebrew 'One the Lord helps'.

Azriel   Hebrew 'Angel of the Lord'.

boys

B

Bachir Arabic 'Welcome'.

Bahar Arabic 'Sailor'.

Bahram Persian 'Ancient king'.

Bailey French 'Steward'. The trusted guardian of other men's properties.
Baillie, Baily, Bayley

Bainbridge Anglo-Saxon 'Bridge over the white water'.

Baird Celtic 'The minstrel'. The ancient bard.
Bard, Barde

Balbo Latin 'The mutterer'.

Baldemar Teutonic 'Bold, famous prince'.

Balder Norse 'Prince'. The god of peace.
Baldhere, Baldur

Baldric Teutonic 'Princely ruler'.
Baudric

Baldwin   Teutonic 'Bold, noble protector'.
Balduin, Baudouin, Baudowin

Balfour   Gaelic 'From the pasture'.

Ballard   Teutonic 'Strong and bold'.

Balraj   Hindi 'Strongest'.

Balthasar   Greek 'May the Lord protect the King'.
Belshazzar

Bancroft   Anglo-Saxon 'From the bean field'.

Banning   Gaelic 'The little golden-haired one'.

Banquo   Gaelic 'White'.

Barak   Hebrew 'Flash of lightning'.

Baram   Hebrew 'Son of the nation'.

Barclay   Anglo-Saxon 'One who lives by the birch tree meadow'.
Berkeley, Berkley

Barden   Old English 'One who lives near the boar's den'.

Bardo   Danish Diminutive of Bartholomew.

Bardolf   Anglo-Saxon 'Axe wolf'.
Bardolph, Bardolphe, Bardulf, Bardulph

Bardon   Anglo-Saxon 'Barley valley'.

Bardrick   Anglo-Saxon 'Axe ruler'. One who lived by the battle axe.
Baldric, Baldrick

Barend   Dutch 'Firm bear'.

Bari   Arabic 'The maker'.

Barker   Old English 'Birch tree'.

Barlow   Anglo-Saxon 'One who lives on the barren hills'.

Barnaby Hebrew 'Son of consolation'.
Barnaba, Barnabe, Barnabus, Barney, Barny

Barnes Old English 'Bear'.

Barnett Anglo-Saxon 'Noble leader'.
Barnet

Barnum Anglo-Saxon 'Nobleman's house'.

Baron Anglo-Saxon 'Noble warrior'. The lowest rank of the peerage.
Barron

Barr Anglo-Saxon 'A gateway'.

Barret Teutonic 'As mighty as the bear'.
Barrett

Barris Celtic 'Barry's son'.

Barry Gaelic 'Spear-like'. One whose intellect is sword-sharp.
Barrie

Bartholomew Hebrew 'Son of the furrows, ploughman'. One of the
12 apostles.
*Bardo, Bart, Bartel, Barth, Barthel, Barthelmey, Barthol,
Bartholomeo, Bartholomeus, Bartlett, Bartley, Bartolome,
Bat, Parlan*

Bartley Anglo-Saxon 'Bartholomew's meadow'.

Barton Anglo-Saxon 'Barley farmer'.
Bartie

Bartram Old German 'Bright raven'.

Baruch Hebrew 'Blessed'.
Barrie, Barry

Barulai Hebrew 'Man of iron'.

Bashir Sanskrit 'Bringer of good news'.

Basil Greek 'Kingly'. St Basil was the founder of the Greek Orthodox Church.
Base, Basile, Basilio, Basilius, Vassily

Basilyr Arabic 'Insight'.

Basum Arabic 'Smiling'.

Baxter Teutonic 'The baker of bread'.
Bax

Bayard Anglo-Saxon 'Red haired and strong'. The personification of knightly courtesy.
Bay

Baylor Anglo-Saxon 'Horse trainer'.

Beacher Anglo-Saxon 'One who lives by the oak tree'.
Beach, Beech, Beecher

Beagan Gaelic 'Little one'.
Beagen

Beal French 'Handsome'. In the form 'Beau' used to identify the smart, well-dressed, personable men of the 17th and early 18th centuries.
Beale, Beall, Beau

Beaman Anglo-Saxon 'The bee keeper'.

Beasley Old English 'Field of peas'.

Beattie Gaelic 'Public provider'. One who supplies food and drink for the inhabitants of a town.
Beatie, Beatty, Beaty

Beaufort French 'Beautiful stronghold'. The name adopted by the descendants of the union of John of Gaunt and Katharine Swynford.

Beaumont French 'Beautiful mountain'.

Beauregard   Old French 'Beautiful in expression'.

Beck   Anglo-Saxon 'A brook'.
Bec

Bede   Old English 'A prayer'.

Bedell   Old English 'Messenger'.

Behram   Persian 'Mythological figure'.

Behzad   Persian 'Noble'.

Belden   Anglo-Saxon 'One who lives in the beautiful glen'.
Beldon

Bellamy   French 'Handsome friend'.

Belton   Old French 'Beautiful town'.

Beltran   German 'Brilliant'.

Bemus   Greek 'Platform'.

Ben   Popular variation of Benjamin.

Benedict   Latin 'Blessed'. One blessed by God.
Ben, Bendick, Bendix, Benedetto, Benedic, Benedick, Benedicto, Benedikt, Benedix, Bengt, Benito, Bennet, Bennett, Benny, Benoit, Benot

Beniah   Hebrew 'Son of the Lord'.

Benjamin   Hebrew 'Son of my right hand'. The beloved youngest son.
Beathan, Ben, Beniamino, Benjie, Benjy, Bennie, Benny, Benyamin

Benoni   Hebrew 'Son of my sorrow'. The former name of the Biblical Benjamin.

Benroy   Hebrew 'Son of a lion'.

Benson   Hebrew 'Son of Benjamin'.

Bently Anglo-Saxon 'From the farm where the grass sways'.
Bentley

Benton Anglo-Saxon 'From the town on the moors'.

Béraud French 'Strong leader'.
Beraut

Berenger Teutonic 'Bear spear'.

Beresford Anglo-Saxon 'From the barley ford'.

Berg Teutonic 'The mountain'.

Berger French 'The shepherd'.

Bernard Teutonic 'As brave as a bear'. A courageous warrior.
Barnard, Barnet, Barnett, Barney, Barny, Bearnard, Berard, Bern, Bernado, Bernhard, Bernie, Berny, Burnard

Berthold Teutonic 'Brilliant ruler'.
Bert, Berthoud, Bertie, Bertold

Berton Anglo-Saxon 'Brilliant one's estate'.
Bertie, Burt, Burton

Bertram Anglo-Saxon 'Bright raven'.
Bartram, Bert, Bertrand, Bertrando

Berwick Old English 'Barley grange'.

Berwin Teutonic 'Warrior friend'.

Bevan Welsh 'Son of a noble man'.
Beavan, Beaven, Beven

Beverley Anglo-Saxon 'From the beaver meadow'.
Beverly

Bevis French 'Fair view'.
Beavais

Bhagat   Arabic 'Joy'.

Bibiano   Spanish   Spanish variation of Vivien.

Bickford   Anglo-Saxon 'Hewer's ford'.

Bienvenido   Spanish 'Welcome'.

Bildad   Hebrew 'Beloved'.

Bing   Teutonic 'Kettle-shaped hollow'.

Bion   Greek 'Life'.

Birch   Anglo-Saxon 'At the birch tree'.
Birk, Burch

Birkett   Anglo-Saxon 'One who lives by the birch headland'.
Birket

Birley   Anglo-Saxon 'Cattle shed in the field'.

Birney   Anglo-Saxon 'One who lives on the island in the brook'.

Birtle   Anglo-Saxon 'From the bird hill'.

Bishop   Anglo-Saxon 'The bishop'.

Bjorn   Scandinavian 'Bear'.

Black   Anglo-Saxon 'Of dark complexion'.

Blade   Anglo-Saxon 'Prosperity, glory'.

Blagden   Anglo-Saxon 'From the dark valley'.

Blagoslav   Polish 'Good glory'.

Blaine   Gaelic 'Thin, hungry-looking'.
Blane, Blain, Blayn, Blayne

Blair   Gaelic 'A place' or 'from the plain'.

Blaise Latin 'Stammerer' or 'firebrand'.
Blase, Blayze, Blaze

Blake Anglo-Saxon 'Of fair complexion'.

Blakey Anglo-Saxon 'Little fair one'.

Bland Latin 'Mild and gentle'.

Blanford Anglo-Saxon 'River crossing belonging to one with grey hair'.
Blandford

Bliss Anglo-Saxon 'Joyful one'. One who always see the cheerful side.

Blythe Anglo-Saxon 'The merry person'.
Blyth

Boaz Hebrew 'Strength is in the Lord'.
Boas, Boase

Boden French 'The herald'. The bringer of news.

Bogart Teutonic 'Strong bow'.

Bogdan Polish 'God's gift'.

Bolton French 'Manor farm'.

Bonamy French 'Good friend'.

Bonar French 'Good, gentle and kind'.

Bonaro Italian/Spanish 'Friend'.

Bond Anglo-Saxon 'Tiller of the soil'.
Bondie, Bondon

Boniface Latin 'One who does good'.

Booker Anglo-Saxon 'Beech tree'.

Boone   Norse 'The good one'.
Boonie

Booth   Teutonic 'From a market' or 'herald'.
Both, Boot, Boote, Boothe

Borden   Anglo-Saxon 'From the valley of the boar'.
Bord

Borg   Norse 'One who lives in the castle'.

Boris   Slavic 'A fighter'. A born warrior.

Bosley   Old English 'Grove of trees'.

Boswell   French 'Forest town'.

Bosworth   Anglo-Saxon 'At the cattle enclosure'.

Botolf   Anglo-Saxon 'Herald wolf'.
Botolph, Botolphe

Boucard   French/Teutonic 'Beech tree'.
Bouchard

Bourne   Anglo-Saxon 'From the brook'.
Bourn, Burn, Burne, Byrne

Bowen   Celtic 'Descendant of Owen'. A proud Welsh name borne by descendants of the almost legendary Owen.

Bowie   Gaelic 'Yellow haired'.
Bow

Boyce   French 'From the woods'. A forester.
Boycie

Boyd   Gaelic 'Light haired'. The blond Adonis.

Boyden   Celtic 'Herald'.

Boyne   Gaelic 'White cow'. A very rare person.

Bradburn Anglo-Saxon 'Broad brook'.

Braden Anglo-Saxon 'From the wide valley'.
Bradan, Brade

Bradford Anglo-Saxon 'From the broad crossing'.

Bradley Anglo-Saxon 'From the broad meadow'.
Brad, Bradly, Bradney, Lee

Bradshaw Old English 'Large virginal forest'.

Brady Gaelic 'Spirited one' or 'from the broad island'.

Brage Nordic 'Norse god of poetry'.

Braham Hindi 'Creator'.

Brainard Anglo-Saxon 'Bold as a raven'. One who knows no fear.
Brainerd

Bramwell Anglo-Saxon 'From the bramble bush spring'.

Bran Celtic 'Raven'. The spirit of eternal youth.
Bram

Brand Anglo-Saxon 'Firebrand'. The grandson of the god Woden.
Brandt, Brantley

Brander Norse 'Sword of fire'.

Brandon Anglo-Saxon 'From the beacon on the hill'.
Brandyn, Brannon

Brant Anglo-Saxon 'Fiery or proud one'.

Brawley Anglo-Saxon 'From the meadow on the hill slope'.

Braxton Anglo-Saxon 'Brock's town'.

Brendan Gaelic 'Little raven' or 'from the fiery hill'.
Bren, Brendis, Brendon, Brennan

Brent Anglo-Saxon 'Steep hill'.

Brett Celtic 'Native of Brittany' or 'from the island of Britain'. One of the original Celts.
Bret, Britt

Brewster Anglo-Saxon 'The brewer'.
Brew

Brian Celtic 'Powerful strength with virtue and honour'. From Brian Boru, the great Irish king.
Briano, Briant, Brien, Brion, Bryan, Bryant, Bryon

Brice Celtic 'Quick, ambitious and alert'.
Bryce

Bridger Anglo-Saxon 'One who lives by the bridge'.

Brigham Anglo-Saxon 'One who lives where the bridge is enclosed'.
Brigg

Brinsley Anglo-Saxon 'Brin's meadow'.

Brock Anglo-Saxon 'The badger'.
Broc, Brockie, Brok

Brockley Anglo-Saxon 'From the badger meadow'.

Broderick Anglo-Saxon 'From the broad ridge' or 'son of Roderick'.
Broderic

Brodie Gaelic 'A ditch'.
Brody

Bromley Anglo-Saxon 'One who lives of the broom meadow'.

Bronislav Slavonic 'Weapon of glory'.

Bronson Anglo-Saxon 'The brown-haired one's son'.
Bronnie

Brook Anglo-Saxon 'One who lives by the brook'.
Brooke, Brooks

Brooklyn American Place name.

Brougher Anglo-Saxon 'The fortified residence'.
Brough

Broughton Anglo-Saxon 'From a fortified town'.

Bruce French 'From the thicket'. From Robert the Bruce, Scotland's hero king.

Bruno Teutonic 'Brown-haired man'.

Brychan Welsh 'Freckled'.

Bryn Welsh 'Hill'.

Buck Anglo-Saxon 'The buck deer'. A fast-running youth.

Buckley Anglo-Saxon 'One who dwells by the buck-deer meadow'.

Budd Anglo-Saxon 'Herald'. The welcome messenger.

Buddy American 'Herald'.

Bundy Anglo-Saxon 'Free man'. An enfranchised serf.

Burbank Anglo-Saxon 'One who lives on the castle hill slope'.

Burchard Anglo-Saxon 'Strong as a castle'.
Burckhard, Burgard, Burkhart

Burdett French 'Little shield'.

Burdon Anglo-Saxon 'One who lives by the castle on the hill'.

Burford Anglo-Saxon 'One who lives at the river crossing by the castle'.

Burgess Anglo-Saxon 'One who lives in a fortified town'.
Berg, Berger, Bergess, Burg

Burke French 'From the stronghold'.
Berk, Berke, Birk, Birke, Bourke, Burk

Burkett French 'From the little fortress'.

Burl Anglo-Saxon 'The cup bearer'. The wine server.
Byrle

Burley Anglo-Saxon 'One who lives in the castle by the meadow'.
Burleigh

Burnaby Norse 'Warrior's estate'.

Burnell French 'Little one with brown hair'.

Burnett Anglo-Saxon 'Little one with brown complexion'.

Burney Anglo-Saxon 'One who lives on the island in the brook'.

Burr Norse 'Youth'.

Burrell French 'One of light brown complexion'.

Burris Old English 'Of the town'.

Burton Anglo-Saxon 'Of bright and glorious fame' or one who lives at the fortified town'.
Bert, Berton, Burt

Busby Norse 'One who lives in the thicket'.

Byford Anglo-Saxon 'One who lives by the ford'.

Byram Anglo-Saxon 'One who lives at the cattle pen'.
Byrom

Byrd Anglo-Saxon 'Like a bird'.

Byron French 'From the cottage' or 'the bear'.
Byran

boys

Cadby Norse 'Warrior's settlement'.

Caddock Celtic 'Keenness in battle'. An eager warrior.

Cadell Celtic 'Battle spirit'.

Cadeyrn Welsh 'Battle king'.

Cadfael Welsh 'Battle metal'.

Cadfan Welsh 'Battle peak'.

Cadman Celtic 'Battle man'.

Cadmus Greek 'Man from the east'. The legendary scholar who devised the Greek alphabet.

Cadogan Celtic 'War'.

Cadwallader Celtic 'Battle leader'.

Cady French 'Simple happiness'.

Caedmon Celtic 'Wise warrior'.

C
boys

Caesar — Latin 'Emperor'. Source of all names meaning Emperor - Tsar, Kaiser, Shah, etc.
Cesar, Cesare

Cain — Hebrew 'The possessed'. The original murderer in the Bible.

Calder — Anglo-Saxon 'The brook'.

Caldwell — Anglo-Saxon 'The cold spring (or well)'.

Caleb — Hebrew 'The bold one'. The impetuous hero.
Cal, Cale

Caley — Gaelic 'Thin, slender'.

Calhoun — Gaelic 'From the forest strip'.

Callum — Celtic 'Dove'.

Calvert — Anglo-Saxon 'One who looks after the calves'.

Calvin — Latin 'Bald'.
Cal, Calvino

Camden — Gaelic 'From the valley which winds'.

Cameron — Celtic 'Crooked nose'. The founder of the Scottish clan.
Cam, Camm, Caney

Camilo — Spanish 'Free born'.

Campbell — Celtic 'Crooked mouth'. Founder of Campbell clan.

Candan — Turkish 'Sincerely, heartily'.

Canute — Norse 'The knot'. Name of the king who tried to hold back the waves.
Knut, Knute

Caradoc — Celtic 'Beloved'.

Carey — Celtic 'One who lives in a castle'.
Care, Cary

Carleton	Anglo-Saxon 'Farmers' meeting place'. *Carl, Carlton*
Carlin	Gaelic 'Little champion'. *Carling*
Carlisle	Anglo-Saxon 'Tower of the castle'. *Carlile, Carlyle, Carlysle*
Carmichael	Celtic 'From St Michael's castle'.
Carmine	Latin 'Song'.
Carney	Gaelic 'Victorious'. The warrior who never lost a battle. *Carny, Kearney*
Carol	Gaelic 'The champion'. The unbeatable fighter. *Carolus, Carrol, Carroll, Caryl*
Carollan	Gaelic 'Little champion'.
Carr	Norse 'One who dwells beside a marsh'. *Karr, Kerr*
Carrick	Gaelic 'The rocky cape'.
Carson	Anglo-Saxon 'Son of the man who lives by the marsh'.
Carswell	Anglo-Saxon 'The watercress grower'.
Carter	Anglo-Saxon 'The cart driver'. One who transports cattle and goods.
Cartland	Celtic 'The land between the rivers'.
Carvell	French 'Estate in the marshes'. *Carvel*
Carver	Old English 'Woodcarver'.
Carvey	Gaelic 'The athlete'. *Carvy*

Casey   Gaelic 'Brave and watchful'. The warrior who never slept.
Case

Casimir   Slavic 'The proclaimer of peace'.
Cass, Cassie, Cassy, Kasimir, Kazimir

Caspar   Persian 'Master of the treasure'. One trusted to guard the most precious possessions.
Casper, Gaspar, Gasper

Cassidy   Gaelic 'Ingenuity' or 'curly haired'.

Cassius   Latin 'Vain and conceited'. Never far from a mirror.
Cash

Castor   Greek 'The beaver'. An industrious person.

Cathmor   Gaelic 'Great warrior'.

Cato   Latin 'The wise one'. One with great worldly knowledge.

Cavan   Gaelic 'Handsome'. The Irish Adonis.
Kavan

Cavell   French 'Little lively one'. Always up and doing.

Cawley   Norse 'Ancestral relic'.

Cecil   Latin 'The unseeing one'.
Cece, Cecilio, Cecilius, Celio, Sissil

Cedric   Celtic 'Chieftain'.
Caddaric

Cephas   Aramaic 'Rock'.

Cerwyn   Welsh 'Fair love'.

Chad   Anglo-Saxon 'War-like, bellicose'.
Cadda, Chadda, Chaddie

Chadwick   Anglo-Saxon 'Town of the warrior'.

Chaim   Hebrew 'Life'.

Chalmer   Celtic 'The chamberlain's son' or 'king of the household'.
Chalmers

Chance   Anglo-Saxon 'Good fortune'.
Chauncey

Chancellor   Anglo-Saxon 'King's counsellor'. Trusted with state secrets.
Chanceller, Chaunceler, Chaunceller, Chauncey

Chander   Sanskrit 'The moon who outshines the stars'.

Chandler   French 'The candle maker'.
Chane

Chaney   French 'Oak wood'.

Channing   French 'The canon'.
Cannon, Chan

Chapman   Anglo-Saxon 'The merchant'. The travelling salesmen of medieval times.

Charles   Teutonic 'The strong man'. The personification of all that is masculine.
Carey, Carl, Carlo, Carlos, Carol, Carrol, Cary, Charlie, Charley, Chas, Chuck, Karl, Karlan, Karlens, Karol, Tearlach

Charlie   Popular variation of Charles.

Charlton   Anglo-Saxon 'Charles's farm'.
Charleton

Chase   French 'The hunter'. One who enjoys the chase.

Chatham   Anglo-Saxon 'Land of the soldier'.

Chauncey   French 'Chancellor, record keeper'. Also variation of Chance and Chancellor.
Chancey, Chaunce

Cheiro Greek 'Hand'.

Cheney French 'One who lives in the oak wood'. A woodman.
Cheyney

Chester Latin 'The fortified camp'.
Ches, Cheston

Chet Thai 'Brother'.

Chetwin Anglo-Saxon 'Cottage dweller by the winding path'.
Chetwyn

Cheung Chinese 'Good luck'.

Chevalier French 'Knight'.
Chevy

Chilton Anglo-Saxon 'From the farm by the spring'.
Chelton, Chilt

Christian Latin 'Believer in Christ, a Christian'.
Chretien, Chris, Christiano, Christie, Christy, Kit, Kristian, Kristin

Christopher Greek 'The Christ carrier'. The man who carried the infant Christ across the river.
Chris, Christoforo, Christoper, Christoph, Christophe, Christophorus, Cristobal, Gillecirosd, Kit, Kester, Kris, Kriss

Chrysander Greek 'Golden man'.

Chung Chinese 'Intelligent'.

Churchill Anglo-Saxon 'One who lives by the church on the hill'.

Cian Gaelic 'The ancient one'. One who lives long.

Ciaran Irish 'Dark haired'.
Keiran

Cicero Latin 'The chick-pea'.

Clare   Latin/Anglo-Saxon 'Famous one' (Latin) or 'bright, illustrious' (Anglo-Saxon).
Clair

Clarence   Latin/Anglo-Saxon 'Famous, illustrious one'.
Clavance

Clark   French 'Wise and learned scholar'.
Clarke, Clerk

Claud   Latin 'The lame one'.
Claude, Claudian, Claudianus, Chlaudio

Clay   Anglo-Saxon 'From the clay pit'.

Clayborne   Anglo-Saxon 'From the brook by the clay pit'.
Claiborn, Claybourne

Clayton   Anglo-Saxon 'From the clay town' or 'mortal man'.
Clayson

Cleary   Gaelic 'The scholar'.

Cleavon   Old English 'Cliff'.

Cledwyn   Welsh 'Blessed sword'.

Clement   Latin 'Kind and merciful'.
Clem, Clemence, Clemens, Clementius, Clemmy, Clim

Cleon   Greek 'Famous'.

Cletus   Greek 'Summoned'.
Cletis

Cleveland   Anglo-Saxon 'From the cliff land'.
Cleve, Clevey

Clifford   Anglo-Saxon 'From the ford by the cliff'.
Clif, Cliff

Clifton Anglo-Saxon 'From the farm by the cliff'.
Clift

Clinton Anglo-Saxon 'From the farm on the headland'.
Clint

Clive Anglo-Saxon 'Cliff'.
Cleeve, Cleve, Clyve

Clovis Teutonic 'Famous warrior'. An early form of Lewis.

Cluny Gaelic 'From the meadow'.

Clydai Welsh 'Fame'.

Clyde Celtic 'Warm' (Welsh Celtic) or 'heard from the distance' (Scots Celtic).
Cly, Clywd

Coburn Old English 'Small stream'.

Cody Old English 'A cushion'.

Coel Welsh 'Trust'.
Cole

Colbert Anglo-Saxon 'Brilliant seafarer' or 'cool and calm'.
Colvert, Culbert

Colby Norse 'From the dark country'.

Coleman Celtic/Anglo-Saxon 'Keeper of the doves' (Celtic) or 'follower of Nicholas' (Anglo-Saxon).
Col, Cole, Colman

Colin Gaelic 'Strong and virile' or 'the young child' or 'victorious army'.
Colan, Cailean, Collin and all derivative of Nicholas

Colley Old English 'Swarthy'.

Collier Anglo-Saxon 'Charcoal merchant'.
Colier, Colis, Collyer, Colyer

Colter Anglo-Saxon 'The colt herder'. A lover of horses.

Colton Anglo-Saxon 'From the dark town'.

Columba Latin 'Dove'.
Colm, Colum

Conan Celtic 'High and mighty' or 'wisely intelligent'.
Con, Conal, Conant, Conn, Connall, Connel, Kynan, Quinn

Conlan Gaelic 'The hero'.
Conlin, Conlon

Connor Old English 'Wise aid'.

Conrad Teutonic 'Brave counsellor'. One who told what was right,
not what the receiver wanted to hear.
*Con, Connie, Conrade, Conrado, Cort, Curt, Konrad, Kort,
Kurt*

Conroy Gaelic 'The wise one'.

Constantine Latin 'Firm and unwavering'. Always constant.
*Conn, Constant, Constantin, Constantino, Costa,
Konstantin, Konstantine*

Conway Gaelic 'Hound of the plain'.

Cooper Anglo-Saxon 'Barrel maker'.
Coop

Corbett French 'The raven'. From the raven device worn by the
ancient Vikings.
Corbet, Corbie, Corbin, Corby

Corcoran Gaelic 'Reddish complexion'.
Corquoran

Cordell French 'Rope maker'.
Cord

Corey Gaelic 'One who lives in a ravine'.
Cory

Cormick Gaelic 'The charioteer'.
Cormac, Cormack

Cornelius Latin 'Battle horn'.
Cornal, Cornall, Cornel, Cornell, Neal, Neil

Corwin French 'Friend of the heart'.
Corwen

Corydon Greek 'The helmeted man'.

Cosmo Greek 'The perfect order of the universe'.
Cosimo, Cosme

Courtenay French 'A place'.
Cort, Cortie, Corty, Court, Courtney, Curt

Courtland Anglo-Saxon 'One who dwelt on the court land'.
Court

Covell Anglo-Saxon 'One who lives in the cave on the hill'.
Covill

Cowan Gaelic 'Hollow in the hillside'.

Coyle Gaelic 'Battle flower'.
Coile

Craddock Celtic 'Abundance of love'.
Caradoc, Caradock

Craig Celtic 'From the stony hill'.
Craggie

Crandell Anglo-Saxon 'One who lives in the valley of the crane'.
Crandall

Crane Old English 'Cry'.

Cranley Anglo-Saxon 'From the crane meadow'.

Cranog Welsh 'Heron'.

Cranston Anglo-Saxon 'From the farmstead where the cranes gather'.

Crawford Anglo-Saxon 'From the crow ford'.
Crowford

Creighton Anglo-Saxon 'From the farm by the creek'.
Crayton, Creigh, Creight, Crichton

Crispin Latin 'Curly haired'. From St Crispin, the patron saint of shoemakers.
Crepin, Crisp, Crispen

Cromwell Anglo-Saxon 'One who lives by a winding spring'.

Crosby Anglo-Saxon/Norse 'One who lives at the crossroads'.
Crosbey, Crosbie

Crosley Anglo-Saxon 'From the meadow with the cross'.

Cullen Gaelic 'Handsome one'.
Cullan, Cullin

Culley Gaelic 'From the woodland'.
Cully

Culver Anglo-Saxon 'Gentle as the dove, peaceful'. The symbol of peace.
Colver

Curran Gaelic 'The resolute hero'. One who would die defending the right.
Curren, Currey, Currie, Curry

Curtis French 'The courteous one'. A gentleman with perfect manners.
Curelo, Curt, Kurt

Cuthbert Anglo-Saxon 'Famous and brilliant'. One famed for his intellect.

Cybard French 'Ruler'.

Cyndeyrn Welsh 'Chief lord'.

Cynfael Welsh 'Chief metal'.

Cynfor Welsh 'Great chief'.

Cyngen Welsh 'Chief son'.

Cynric Anglo-Saxon 'From the royal line of kings'.

Cynyr Welsh 'Chief hero'.

Cyprian Greek 'Man from Cyprus'.
Ciprian, Cyprien

Cyrano Greek 'From Cyrene'.
Cyrenaica

Cyril Greek 'The lord'.
Cirilo, Cyrill, Cyrille, Cyrillus

Cyrus Persian 'The sun god'. The founder of the Persian Empire.
Ciro

Dabert   French 'Bright action'.

Dacey   Gaelic 'The southerner'.
Dacy

Dag   Norse 'Day of brightness'.

Dagan   Semitic 'The earth' or 'the small fish'.
Dagon

Dagwood   Anglo-Saxon 'Forest of the shining one'.

Dahab   Arabic 'Gold'.

Daimon   Latin 'Guardian angel'.

Dakota   American 'Friend, partner'. Tribal name.

Dalbert   Anglo-Saxon 'From the shining valley'.
Delbert

Dale   Teutonic 'One who lives in the valley'.
Dael

Dallas   Celtic 'Skilled' or 'from the water field'.
Dal, Dallia

Dalston   Old English 'From Daegal's place'.
Dallon

Dalton   Anglo-Saxon 'From the farm in the valley'.
Dalt

Daly   Gaelic 'The counsellor'.

Dalziel   Celtic 'From the little field'.
Dalziell

Daman   Sanskrit 'One in control'.
Damian

Damek   Slavic 'Man of the earth'.

Damon   Greek 'Tame and domesticated'. The true friend.
Damian, Damiano, Damien

Danby   Norse 'From the settlement of the Danish'.

Daniel   Hebrew 'The lord is my judge'.
Dan, Dane, Daniell, Danielle, Danny

Darby   Gaelic 'Freeman'.
Derby

Darcy   French 'From the fortress'.
Darcie, D'Arcy, Darsey, Darsy

Darien   Spanish A place name.

Darius   Greek 'The wealthy man'.
Dare, Dario

Darnell   French 'From the hidden nook'.
Darnall

Darrell   French 'Beloved one'.
Darryl, Daryl, Derril

Darren   Gaelic 'Little great one'.
Daren, Darin, Daron, Derron

Darton Anglo-Saxon 'From the deer forest'.

Darwin Old English 'Beloved friend'.

David Hebrew 'The beloved one'. The patron saint of Wales.
Dave, Daven, Davidson, Davie, Davon, Davy

Davin Scandinavian 'Brightness of the Finns'.

Davis Anglo-Saxon David's son.

De Witt Flemish 'Fair-haired one'.

Dean Anglo-Saxon 'From the valley'.
Deane, Dene, Dino

Dearborn Anglo-Saxon 'Beloved child' or 'from the deer brook'.

Declan Irish 'Man of prayer'.

Dedrick Teutonic 'Ruler of the people'.

Dekkel Arabic 'Palm tree'.

Delaney Gaelic 'Descendant of the challenger'.

Delano French 'From the nut tree woods'.

Delling Norse 'Very shining one'.

Delmar Latin 'From the sea'.
Delmer, Delmor, Delmore

Delwyn Anglo-Saxon 'Bright friend from the valley'.
Delwin

Demas Greek 'The popular person'.

Demetrius Greek 'Belonging to Demeter'.
Demetri, Demetris, Demmy, Dimitri, Dmitri

Demos Greek 'The spokesman of the people'.

Dempsey Gaelic 'The proud one'.

Dempster Anglo-Saxon 'The judge'.

Denby Norse 'From the Danish settlement'.

Denholm Scottish 'Island valley'.

Denley Anglo-Saxon 'One who lives in the meadow in the valley'.

Denman Anglo-Saxon 'Resident in the valley'.

Dennis Greek 'Wine lover'. From Dionysus, the god of wine.
Den, Denis, Dennie, Dennison, Denny, Deny, Denys, Denzil, Dion, Dionisio, Dionysus

Dennison Anglo-Saxon 'Son of Dennis'.
Denison

Denton Anglo-Saxon 'From the farm in the valley'.

Denver Anglo-Saxon 'From the edge of the valley'.

Denzil Cornish 'High stronghold'.

Deodatus Latin 'God-given'.

Derek Teutonic 'Ruler of the people'.
Darrick, Derk, Derrick, Derry, Dirk

Dermot Gaelic 'Free man'.
Diarmid

Derry Gaelic 'The red one'.

Derward Anglo-Saxon 'Guardian of the deer'.

Derwin Anglo-Saxon 'Dearest friend'.

Desmond Gaelic 'Man of the world, sophisticated'.
Desmund

Deverell Celtic 'From the river bank'.

Devin Celtic 'A poet'.

Devlin   Gaelic 'Fierce bravery'.
Devland

Devon   English 'From Devon'. Someone born in that county, the name of which means 'people of the deep valley'.

Dewey   Celtic 'The beloved one'. The Celtic form of David.
Dew

Dexter   Latin 'The right-handed man, dextrous'.
Decca, Deck, Dex

Diamond   Anglo-Saxon 'The shining protector'.

Digby   Norse 'From the settlement by the dyke'.

Diggory   French 'Strayed, lost'.

Dillon   Gaelic 'Faithful'. A true and loyal man.

Dinar   Sanskrit 'Golden coin'.

Dinsdale   English 'Settlement surrounded by a moat'.

Dinsmore   Gaelic 'From the fortified hill'.

Diomede   Greek 'Divine ruler'.

Dixon   Anglo-Saxon 'Son of Richard' (Dick's son).
Dickson

Doane   Celtic 'From the sand dune'.

Dodd   Teutonic 'Of the people'.

Dolan   Gaelic 'Black haired'.

Dominic   Latin 'Belonging to the Lord, born on the Lord's day'.
Dom, Domenico, Domingo, Dominic, Dominik, Dominy, Nic, Nick, Nickie, Nicky

Donahue   Gaelic 'Warrior dressed in brown'.
Don, Donn

Donald Celtic 'Ruler of the world'. The founder of MacDonald clan.
Don, Donal, Donn, Donnall, Donalt, Donaugh, Donnell, Donnie, Donny

Donato Latin 'A gift'.

Donnelly Gaelic 'Brave dark man'.

Donovan Irish 'Dark brown'.

Doran Celtic 'The stranger'.

Dorian Greek 'Man from Doria'.

Dory French 'The golden-haired boy'.

Douglas Celtic 'From the dark stream'. One of the largest Scottish clans.
Doug, Dougal, Douggie, Douggy, Dugal, Dugald, Duggie, Duggy, Duglass

Dow Gaelic 'Black haired'.

Doyle Gaelic 'The dark-haired stranger'.

Drake Anglo-Saxon 'The dragon'.

Drew Celtic 'The wise one'. Also diminutive of Andrew.
Drud

Driscoll Celtic 'The interpreter'.
Driscol

Druce Celtic 'Son of Drew'.

Drury French 'The dear one'.

Dryden Anglo-Saxon 'From the dry valley'.

Dudley Anglo-Saxon 'From the people's meadow'.
Dud, Duddie, Duddy, Dudly

Duff Gaelic 'Dark complexion'.

Dugan Gaelic 'Dark skinned'. The sun-tanned man.
Doogan, Dougan

Duke French 'The leader'.

Dulal Sanskrit 'Precious one'.

Duncan Celtic 'Brown warrior'.
Dunc

Dunham Celtic 'Dark man'.

Dunley Anglo-Saxon 'From the meadow on the hill'.

Dunmore Celtic 'From the fortress on the hill'.

Dunn Anglo-Saxon 'Dark skinned'.

Dunstan Anglo-Saxon 'From the brown stone hill'.

Durant Latin 'Enduring'. One whose friendship is lasting.
Dante, Durand

Durward Anglo-Saxon 'The gate keeper'. The guardian of the drawbridge.

Durwin Anglo-Saxon 'Dear friend'.
Durwyn

Dustin Old German 'Valiant fighter'.
Dustan, Dusty

Dwayne Celtic/Gaelic 'The singer' (Celtic) or 'the small, dark man' (Gaelic).
Dewain, Duane, Dwain

Dwight Teutonic 'The light-haired one'.

Dyfan Welsh 'Tribe ruler'.

Dylan Welsh 'Man from the sea'.
Dilan, Dilly

Dynawd Welsh 'Given'.

boys

E

Eachan   Gaelic 'Little horse'.
Eacheann

Earl   Anglo-Saxon 'Nobleman, chief'.
Erle, Earle, Erl, Errol, Early

Eaton   Anglo-Saxon 'From the estate by the river'.

Eben   Hebrew 'Stone'.

Ebenezer   Hebrew 'Stone of help'.

Edan   Celtic 'Flame'.

Edbert   Anglo-Saxon 'Prosperous, brilliant'.

Edel   Teutonic 'The noble one'.

Edelmar   Anglo-Saxon 'Noble and famous'.

Eden   Hebrew 'Place of delight and pleasure'. The original paradise.

Edgar   Anglo-Saxon 'Lucky spear warrior'.
Ed, Eddie, Eddy, Edgard, Ned

Edlin Anglo-Saxon 'Prosperous friend'.

Edmund Anglo-Saxon 'Rich guardian'.
Eamonn, Ed, Eddie, Eddy, Edmon, Edmond, Edmondo, Edmonn, Ned

Edolf Anglo-Saxon 'Prosperous wolf'.

Edric Anglo-Saxon 'Fortunate ruler'.

Edryd Welsh 'Restoration'.

Edsel Anglo-Saxon 'A prosperous man's house' or 'profound thinker'.

Edson Anglo-Saxon 'Edward's son'.
Edison

Edwald Anglo-Saxon 'Prosperous ruler'.

Edward Anglo-Saxon 'Prosperous guardian'.
Ed, Eddie, Eddy, Edouard, Eduard, Ewart, Ned, Neddie, Neddy, Teddy

Edwin Anglo-Saxon 'Prosperous friend'.
Edd, Eddie, Eddy, Edlin, Eduino

Edwy Old English 'Richly beloved'.

Egan Gaelic 'Formidable, fiery'.
Egon

Egbert Anglo-Saxon 'Bright, shining sword'. The name of the first king of all England.
Bert

Egerton Old English 'Town on ridge'.

Ehren Teutonic 'Honourable one'.

Einar Norse 'Warrior leader'.

Eiros Welsh 'Bright'.

Elaeth Welsh 'Intelligent'.

Elan Hebrew 'Tree'.

Elazar Hebrew 'God helps'.

Elden Anglo-Saxon 'Elf valley'.

Elder Anglo-Saxon 'One who lives by an elder tree'.

Eldon Teutonic/Anglo-Saxon 'Respected elder' (Teutonic) or 'from the holy hill' (Anglo-Saxon).

Eldridge Anglo-Saxon 'Wise adviser'.
Eldred, Eldredge, Eldrid, Eldwin, Eldwyn

Eldwin Old English 'Old friend'.

Eleazar Hebrew 'Helped by God'.
Elizer, Lazar, Lazarus

Eleutherios Greek 'A free man'.

Elfed Welsh 'Autumn'.

Elgar Old English Noble spearman'.

Elhanan Hebrew 'God is gracious'.

Eli Hebrew 'The highest'.
Ely

Elian Hebrew 'Bright'.

Elias Hebrew 'The Lord is God'.
Elihu, Elijah, Eliot, Elliott, Ellis

Elidr Welsh 'Brass'.

Elisha Hebrew 'God is my salvation'.

Elkanah Hebrew 'God has created'.

Ellard Anglo-Saxon 'Noble, brave'.

Ellery Teutonic 'From the elder tree'.
Elery, Ellerey

Ellison Anglo-Saxon 'Son of Elias'.
Elson

Ellsworth Anglo-Saxon 'A farmer, lover of the land'.

Elmer Anglo-Saxon 'Noble, famous'.
Aylmer

Elmo Greek/Italian 'Friendly protector'.

Elmore Anglo-Saxon 'One who lives by the elm tree on the moor'.

Elnathan Hebrew 'God gives'.

Elner Teutonic 'Famous'.

Elon Hebrew 'Sturdy oak'.

Elrad Hebrew 'God is my ruler'.

Elroy French 'The king'. The name is supposed to be an anagram of 'le roi' or it may be from the Spanish 'el rey', both meaning 'the king'.

Elsdon Anglo-Saxon 'Hill belonging to the noble one'.

Elston Anglo-Saxon 'Estate of the noble one'.

Elsworth Anglo-Saxon 'Estate of the noble one'.

Elton Anglo-Saxon 'From the old farm'.

Elvis Norse 'All wise'. The prince of wisdom.

Elvy Anglo-Saxon 'Elfin warrior'. Though small in stature he had the heart of a lion.

Elwell Anglo-Saxon 'From the old well'.

Elwin Anglo-Saxon 'Friend of the elves'.

E
boys

Elwood Anglo-Saxon 'From an ancient forest'.

Emery Teutonic 'Industrious ruler' or 'joint ruler'.
Amerigo, Emerson, Emmerich, Emmery, Emory, Merrick

Emil Teutonic 'Industrious'.
Emelen, Emile, Emilio, Emlen, Emlyn

Emlyn Welsh 'One who lives on the border'.

Emmanuel Hebrew 'God is with us'.
Emanuel, Immanuel, Mannie, Manny, Mano, Manolo, Manuel

Emmet Anglo-Saxon 'The industrious ant'.
Emmett, Emmit, Emmot, Emmott, Emmy

Emry Welsh 'Honour'.

Endemon Greek 'Fortunate'.

Endimion Greek 'Mythological figure, son of Jupiter and Calyce (nymph), so beautiful, honest and just, Jupiter made him immortal'.

Engelbert Old German 'Bright as an angel'.

Ennis Gaelic 'The only choice'.

Enoch Hebrew 'Consecrated, dedicated, devoted'.

Enos Hebrew 'The mortal'.

Ephraim Hebrew 'Abounding in fruitfulness'.
Efrem, Eph

Erasmus Greek 'Worthy of being loved'.
Erasme, Ras, Rasmus

Erastus Greek 'The beloved'.
Ras

Erdogan Turkish 'Son is born'.

Erhard Old German 'Honour'.
Erhart

Eric Norse 'All-powerful ruler' or 'kingly'.
Erich, Erick, Erik, Rick, Ricky

Erin Gaelic 'Peace'.

Erland Anglo-Saxon 'Land of the nobleman'.

Erling Anglo-Saxon 'Son of the nobleman'.

Ernest Anglo-Saxon 'Sincere and earnest'.
Ernesto, Ernestus, Ernie, Ernst, Erny

Erskine Celtic 'From the cliff's height'.

Ervand Scandinavian 'Sea warrior'.

Erwin Old English 'Army friend'.

Esmond Anglo-Saxon 'Gracious protector'.

Este Italian 'Man from the East'.
Estes

Estevan Greek 'Crown'.

Ethan Hebrew 'Steadfast and firm'.
Etan

Ethelbert Teutonic 'Noble, bright'.

Ethelred Teutonic 'Noble counsel'.

Euclid Greek 'True glory'.

Eugene Greek 'Nobly born'.
Eugenio, Eugenius, Gene

Eurwyn Welsh 'Golden and fair'.

Eusebius   Greek 'Honourable'.

Eustace   Greek 'Stable, tranquil' or 'fruitful'.
Eustazio, Eustis

Evan   Gaelic 'Well-born young warrior'. Also Welsh form of John.
Evyn, Ewan, Ewen, Owen

Evaristus   Greek 'Most excellent'.

Evelyn   English From a surname.

Everard   Anglo-Saxon 'Strong as a boar'.
Eb, Eberhard, Eberhart, Ev, Evelin, Evered, Everettt, Ewart

Everley   Anglo-Saxon 'Field of the wild boar'.

Evner   Turkish 'House'.

Ewald   Anglo-Saxon 'The power of the law'.

Ewert   Anglo-Saxon 'Ewe herder'. One who tended the ewes in lamb.

Ewing   Anglo-Saxon 'Friend of the law'.

Eymer   Teutonic 'Royal worker'.

Ezekiel   Hebrew 'Strength of God'.
Zeke

Ezio   Italian 'Aquiline nose'.
Enzio

Ezra   Hebrew 'The one who helps'.
Esra, Ez

F

Fabian Latin 'The bean grower' or 'prosperous farmer'.
Fabe, Faber, Fabiano, Fabien, Fabio

Fabron French 'The little blacksmith'.
Faber, Fabre

Fadoul Arabic 'Honest'.

Fagan Gaelic 'Little, fiery one'.
Fagin

Fai Chinese 'Beginning'.

Fairchild Teutonic 'Fair-haired child'.

Fairfax Anglo-Saxon 'Fair-haired one'.

Fairley Anglo-Saxon 'From the far meadow'.
Fairly, Fairlie, Farl, Farley

Faisal Arabic 'Wise judge'.

Falah Arabic 'Success'.

Falkner Anglo-Saxon 'Falcon trainer'. One who trained the birds used in the hunt.
Faulkener, Faulkner, Fowler

Fane Anglo-Saxon 'Glad, joyful'.

Faramond Teutonic 'Journey protection'.

Farand Teutonic 'Pleasant and attractive'.
Farant, Farrand, Ferrand

Farland Old English 'Land near road'.

Farley Old English 'From the bull meadow'.
Fairleigh, Farleigh

Farnham Teutonic 'Village in the ferns'.

Farnell Anglo-Saxon 'From the fern slope'.
Farnall, Fernald, Fernall

Farnley Anglo-Saxon 'From the fern meadow'.
Fernley

Farold Anglo-Saxon 'Mighty traveller'.

Farquhar Celtic 'Man' or 'friendly'.

Farr Anglo-Saxon 'The traveller'.

Farrell Celtic 'The valorous one'.
Farrel, Ferrell

Faust Latin 'Lucky, auspicious'.

Favian Latin 'A man of understanding'.

Fawaz Arabic 'Victorious'.

Faxon Teutonic 'Thick haired'.

Fay Gaelic 'The raven'. Symbol of great wisdom.
Fayette

Fayad Arabic 'Generous'.

Faysal Arabic 'Decision maker'.

Fayza Arabic 'Victorious'.

Felix Latin 'Fortunate'.
Felice, Felicio, Felizio

Felton Anglo-Saxon 'From the town estate'.

Fenton Anglo-Saxon 'One who lives of the marshland'.

Fenwick Latin 'From the marshland'.

Fenwood Latin 'One who lives in the low-lying forest'.

Ferdinand Teutonic 'Bold, daring adventurer'.
Ferd, Ferdie, Ferdy, Fernand, Fernando, Hernando

Ferdusi Persian 'Paradisical'.

Fergus Gaelic 'The best choice'.
Feargus, Fergie, Ferguson

Fermin Spanish 'Firm'.

Ferrand French 'One with iron grey hair'.
Ferand, Ferant, Ferrant

Ferris Gaelic 'The rock'.
Farris

Festus Latin 'Happy one'.

Fidel Latin 'Advocate of the poor'.
Fidele, Fidelio

Fielding Anglo-Saxon 'One who lives near the field'.

Filbert Anglo-Saxon 'Very brilliant one'.
Filberto, Philbert

Filmer   Anglo-Saxon 'Very famous one'.
Fillmore, Filmore

Fingal   Scottish 'Blond stranger'.

Finlay   Gaelic 'Fair soldier'.
Fin, Findlay, Findley, Finley, Lee

Finn   Gaelic 'Fair haired'.

Firman   Anglo-Saxon 'Long-distance traveller'.
Farman

Firmin   French 'The firm, strong one'.

Fiske   Anglo-Saxon 'Fish'.

Fitch   Anglo-Saxon 'The marten'.

Fitz   Anglo-French 'Son'. Originally in the form of 'fils' (French for son), the present form was introduced into Britain by the Normans.

Fitzgerald   Anglo-Saxon 'Son of Gerald'.

Fitzhugh   Anglo-Saxon 'Son of Hugh'.

Fitzroy   French 'King's son'.

Flann   Gaelic 'Lad with red hair'.

Flavius   Latin 'Yellow-haired one'.
Flavian

Fleming   Anglo-Saxon 'The Dutchman'.
Flem

Fletcher   French 'The arrow maker'.
Fletch

Flinn   Gaelic 'Son of the red-haired one'.
Flynn

Flint Anglo-Saxon 'A stream'.

Florian Latin 'Flowering, blooming'.
Flory

Forbes Gaelic 'Man of prosperity, owner of many fields'. The great landowner.

Ford Anglo-Saxon 'The river crossing'.

Forrest Teutonic 'Guardian of the forest'.
Forest, Forester, Forrester, Forrie, Forster, Foss, Foster

Fortune French 'The lucky one'. Child of many blessings.

Francis Latin 'Free man'.
Fran, Franchot, Frank, Frankie, Franz

Franklin Anglo-Saxon 'Free-holder of property'. One who owned his own land to use as he wished.
Francklin, Francklyn, Frank, Frankie, Franklyn

Fraser French 'Strawberry' or 'curly-haired one'.
Frasier, Frazer, Frazier

Frayne Anglo-Saxon 'Stranger'.
Fraine, Frean, Freen, Freyne

Frederick Teutonic 'Peaceful ruler'. One who used diplomacy not war.
Fred, Freddie, Freddy, Frederic, Frederik, Fredric, Fredrick, Friedrich, Fritz

Freeland Old English 'From free land'.

Freeman Anglo-Saxon 'Born a free man'.
Freedman

Fremont Teutonic 'Free and noble protector'.

Frewin Anglo-Saxon 'Free, noble friend'.
Frewen

Frey   Anglo-Saxon 'The lord of peace and prosperity'. From the ancient Norse god.

Frick   Anglo-Saxon 'Bold man'.

Fridolf   Anglo-Saxon 'Peaceful wolf'.

Fulbright   Old German 'Very bright'.
Fulbert

Fuller   Anglo-Saxon 'One who works with cloth'.
Tucker

Fulton   Anglo-Saxon 'From the field' or 'living by the chicken pen'.

Fyfe   Scottish 'Man from Fife'.
Fife, Fyffe

boys

Gable French 'The small Gabriel'.

Gabriel Hebrew 'Messenger of God'. The archangel who announced the birth of Christ.
Gabbie, Gabby, Gabe, Gabie, Gabriello

Gage French 'A pledge'. The glove that was given as an earnest of good faith.

Gair Gaelic 'Short one'.

Gaius Latin 'Rejoiced'.

Galdemar French/Old German 'Famous ruler'.

Gale Celtic 'The lively one'.
Gail, Gayle

Galen Gaelic/Greek 'Little bright one' or 'helper'.
Gaelen

Gallagher Gaelic 'Eager helper from overseas'.

Galloway Celtic 'Man from the stranger lands'.
Gallway, Galway

Galpin Old French 'Runner'.

Galt Old English 'High land'.

Galton Anglo-Saxon 'Lease holder of an estate'.

Galvin Gaelic 'Bright, shining white', or 'the sparrow'.
Galvan, Galven

Gamalat Arabic 'Beautiful one'.

Gamaliel Hebrew 'The recompense of the Lord'.

Gannon Gaelic 'Little blond one'.

Ganymede Greek 'Rejoicing in mankind'.

Gardiner Teutonic 'A gardener, a flower lover'.
Gardener, Gardner

Gareth Welsh 'Gentle'.

Garfield Anglo-Saxon 'War or battle field'.

Garland Anglo-Saxon 'From the land of the spears'.

Garman Anglo-Saxon 'The spearman'.

Garmond Anglo-Saxon 'Spear protector'.
Garmon, Garmund

Garner Teutonic 'Army guard, noble defender'.

Garnet Latin 'A red seed, pomegranate seed'.

Garnett Anglo-Saxon 'Compulsive spear man'. One who struck first and challenged afterwards.

Garnock Celtic 'One who dwells by the river alder'.

Garrett Anglo-Saxon 'Mighty spear warrior'.
Garett, Garrard, Garret, Garritt, Gerard, Jarrett

Garrick Anglo-Saxon 'Spear ruler'.
Garek, Garrek

Garroway Anglo-Saxon 'Spear warrior'.
Garraway

Garson French 'Young man' or 'garrison'.

Garth Norse 'From the garden'.

Garton Anglo-Saxon 'The one who lives by the triangular-shaped farm'.

Garvey Gaelic 'Rough peace'. Peace obtained after victory.
Garvie

Garvin Teutonic 'Spear friend'.
Garwin

Garwood Anglo-Saxon 'From the fir trees'.

Gary Anglo-Saxon 'Spearman'.
Gare, Garey, Gari, Garry

Gaspar Persian 'Master of the treasure'. One of the Magi.
Caspar, Casper, Gasper, Jasper, Kaspar, Kasper

Gaston French 'Man from Gascony'.

Gaubert Old German 'Brilliant ruler'.

Gauderic Old German 'Ruler, king'.

Gawain Celtic 'The battle hawk'.
Gavan, Gaven, Gavin, Gawaine, Gawen

Gaylord French 'The happy noble man'.
Gallard, Galor, Gayler

Gaynor Gaelic 'Son of the blond-haired one'.

Geary Anglo-Saxon 'Changeable'.
Gearey, Gery

Gemmel Scandinavian 'Old'.

Geoffrey Teutonic 'God's Divine peace'.
Geof, Geoff, Godfrey, Jeff, Jeffers, Jeffery, Jeffrey, Jeffry

George Greek 'The farmer'. The patron saint of England.
Geordie, Georg, Georges, Georgie, Georgy, Giorgio, Gordie, Gordy, Jorge, Jorgen, Jorin, Joris, Jurgen, Yorick

Geraint Welsh 'Old'.

Gerald Teutonic 'Mighty spear ruler'.
Garold, Gearalt, Ger, Geraud, Gereld, Gerrald, Gerry, Gery, Giraldo, Giraud, Jer, Jerald, Jereld, Jerold, Jerrold, Jerry

Gerard Anglo-Saxon 'Spear strong, spear brave'.
Gearard, Gerardo, Gerhard, Gerhardt, Gerrard, Gerry

Gervase Teutonic 'Spear vassal'.
Ger, Gervais, Jarv, Jarvey, Jarvis, Jervis, Jervoise

Gerwyn Welsh 'Fair love'.

Gethin Welsh 'Dark skinned'.

Ghislaine French 'A pledge'.

Gibson Anglo-Saxon 'Son of Gilbert'.

Gideon Hebrew 'Brave indomitable spirit' or 'the destroyer'.

Gifford Teutonic 'The gift'.
Giffard, Gifferd

Gilbert Anglo-Saxon 'Bright pledge' or 'a hostage'.
Bert, Gib, Gibb, Gil, Gilibeirt, Gill, Gilleabart, Gillie

Gilby Norse 'The pledge' or 'a hostage'.
Gilbey

Gilchrist Gaelic 'The servant of Christ'.
Gilecriosd

Giles Latin/French 'Shield bearer'.
Gil, Gilles

Gilman Teutonic 'Big man'.

Gilmer Anglo-Saxon 'Famous hostage'. An eminent knight taken captive in battle.

Gilmore Gaelic 'Mary's servant'.
Gillmore, Gilmour

Gilroy Latin/Gaelic 'The king's servant'.

Girvin Gaelic 'Little rough one'.
Girvan, Girven

Gladwin Anglo-Saxon 'Kind friend'.

Glanville French 'One who lives on the oak tree estate'.
Glanvil

Glen Celtic 'From the valley'.
Glenn, Glyn, Glynn

Glendon Celtic 'From the fortress in the glen'.
Glenden

Goddard Teutonic 'Divinely firm'. Firm in belief and trust in God.
Godard, Godart, Goddart

Golding Anglo-Saxon 'Son of the golden one'.

Goldwin Anglo-Saxon 'Golden friend'.

Gomez Spanish 'Man'.

Goodman Anglo-Saxon 'Good man'.

Goodwin Anglo-Saxon 'Good friend' or 'God's friend'.
Godewyn, Godwin, Godwine

Gordon Anglo-Saxon 'From the cornered hill'.
Gordan, Gorden, Gordie, Gordy

Gorham Old English 'One who lives in the mud hut'.

Gorman Gaelic 'Small, blue-eyed boy'.

Gouveneur French 'The governor, the ruler'.

Gower Celtic 'The pure one'.

Grady Gaelic 'Illustrious and noble'.

Graham Teutonic 'From the grey lands'. One from the country beyond the mists.
Graeme

Granger Anglo-Saxon 'The farmer'.
Grange

Grant French 'The great one'.
Grantley, Grenville

Grantham Old English 'From the big meadow'.

Granville French 'One who lives in the big town'.
Grandvil, Grandville, Granvil, Greville

Grayson Anglo-Saxon 'The bailiff's son'.

Greeley Anglo-Saxon 'From the grey meadow'.

Gregory Greek 'The watchful one'. Someone ever vigilant.
Greagoir, Greg, Gregg, Gregor, Gregorio, Gregorius, Greiogair

Gresham Anglo-Saxon 'From the grazing meadow'.

Griffith Celtic 'Fierce red-haired warrior'.
Griffin, Gruffydd, Rufus

Griswold Teutonic 'From the grey forest'.

Grosvenor   Old French   'Great hunter'.

Grover   Anglo-Saxon   'One who comes from the grove'.

Guillym   Welsh   Welsh form of William.

Gunther   Teutonic   'Bold warrior'.
Gunar, Gunnar, Gunner, Guntar, Gunter, Gunthar

Gustave   Scandinavian   'Staff of the Goths'.
Gus, Gustaf, Gustav, Gustavo, Gustavus

Guthrie   Celtic   'War serpent, war hero' or 'from the windy country'.
Guthry

Guy   Latin/French/Teutonic   'Life' (Latin), 'guide' (French) or 'warrior' (Teutonic).
Guido, Guyon, Wiatt, Wyatt

Gwynfor   Welsh   'Fair place'.

Gwynllyw   Welsh   'Blessed leader'.

Gwynn   Celtic   'The blond one'.
Guin

H

Haakon Scandinavian 'Noble kin'.

Haaris Arabic 'Vigilant'.

Hackett Teutonic 'The small woodsman'. The apprentice forester.
Hacket

Hacon Old Norse 'Useful'.

Hadar Hebrew 'Ornament'.

Hadden Anglo-Saxon 'From the heath valley'.
Haddan, Haddon

Hadi Arabic 'Guide'.

Hadley Anglo-Saxon 'From the hot meadow'.
Had, Hadlee, Hadleigh

Hadwin Anglo-Saxon 'Battle companion'.

Hafiz Arabic 'He who remembers'.

Hagen Gaelic 'The young one'.
Hagan, Haggan, Haggen

Hagley Anglo-Saxon 'From the hedged meadow'.

Hagos Ethiopian 'Happy'.

Haig Anglo-Saxon 'One who lives in an enclosure'.

Hakeem Arabic 'Wise'.
Hakim

Hakon Norse 'From an exalted race'.
Haakon, Hako

Halbert Anglo-Saxon 'Brilliant hero'.

Halden Norse 'Half Danish'.
Haldan, Haldane, Halfdan

Hale Anglo-Saxon 'From the hall'.

Haley Gaelic 'The ingenious one'. One with a scientific intelligence.

Halford Anglo-Saxon 'From the ford by the manor house'.

Halim Arabic 'Patient'.

Hall Anglo-Saxon 'One who lives at the manor house'.

Hallam Anglo-Saxon 'One who lives on the hill slopes'.

Halley Anglo-Saxon 'From the manor house meadow' or 'holy'.

Halliwell Anglo-Saxon 'The one who lives by the holy well'.

Hallward Anglo-Saxon 'Guardian of the manor house'.
Halward

Halsey Anglo-Saxon 'From Hal's island'.
Halsy

Halstead Anglo-Saxon 'From the manor house'.
Halsted

Halton Anglo-Saxon 'From the estate on the hill slope'.

Ham   Hebrew 'South'.

Hamal   Arabic 'The lamb'. A very gentle person.

Hamar   Norse 'Symbol of ingenuity'. A great gift for invention.
Hammar

Hamilton   French/Anglo-Saxon 'From the mountain village'.
Hamil

Hamlet   Teutonic 'Little village'.

Hamlin   Teutonic 'Small home lover'.
Hamelin, Hamelyn, Hamlyn

Hamon   Greek 'Faithful'.

Hanafi   Arabic 'Orthodox'.

Hanan   Hebrew 'Grace'.

Hanford   Anglo-Saxon 'From the high ford'.

Hanif   Arabic 'Orthodox, true'.

Hanley   Anglo-Saxon 'From the high meadow'.
Handley, Henleigh, Henley

Hannibal   Greek The hero of Carthage.

Hansel   Scandinavian 'Gift from the Lord'.

Harcourt   French 'From a fortified court'.

Harden   Anglo-Saxon 'From the valley of the hare'.

Harding   Anglo-Saxon 'Son of the hero'.

Hardwin   Anglo-Saxon 'Brave friend'.
Haarwyn, Hardwyn, Harwin

Hardy   Teutonic 'Bold and daring'.
Hardey, Hardi, Hardie

Harford   Anglo-Saxon 'From the hare ford'.
Hareford, Hereford, Herford

Hargrove   Anglo-Saxon 'From the hare grove'.
Hargrave, Hargreave, Hargreaves

Harley   Anglo-Saxon 'From the hare meadow'.
Arley, Arlie, Harden, Harl, Harleigh, Hart, Hartleigh, Hartley

Harlon   Teutonic 'From the battle land'.
Harlan, Harland

Harlow   Anglo-Saxon 'The fortified hill'. An army camp on the hillside.

Harold   Anglo-Saxon 'Army commander'. A mighty general.
Araldo, Hal, Harailt, Harald, Harry, Herald, Herold, Herrick

Harper   Anglo-Saxon 'The harp player'. The wandering minstrel.

Harrison   Anglo-Saxon 'Harold's son'.
Harris

Harry   Popular variation of Henry.

Hart   Anglo-Saxon 'The hart deer'.

Hartford   Anglo-Saxon 'The river crossing of the deer'.
Hertford

Hartwell   Anglo-Saxon 'Well where the deer drink'.
Harwell, Hart, Hartwill, Harwill

Hartwood   Anglo-Saxon 'Forest of the hart deer'.
Harwood

Harvey   Teutonic/French 'Army warrior'.
Harv, Harve, Herv, Herve, Hervey

Hashim   Arabic 'Destroyer of evil'.
Hasheem

Hassan   Arabic 'Handsome'.

Hastings   Anglo-Saxon 'Son of violence'.

Havelock   Norse 'Sea battle'.
Havlock

Haven   Anglo-Saxon 'A place of safety'.

Hawley   Anglo-Saxon 'From the hedged meadow'.

Hayden   Teutonic 'From the hedged valley'.
Haydon

Hayes   Old English 'From the hedged forest'.

Hayward   Anglo-Saxon 'Keeper of the hedged field'.
Heyward

Haywood   Anglo-Saxon 'From the hedged forest'.
Heywood

Heath   Anglo-Saxon 'Heathland'.

Heathcliff   Anglo-Saxon 'From the heather cliff'.
Heathcliffe

Hector   Greek 'Steadfast, unswerving, holds fast'.
Eachan, Eachann, Eachunn, Heck

Hedley   Old English 'Blessed peace'.

Henderson   Old English 'Son of Henry'.

Henry   Teutonic 'Ruler of the estate'. Lord of the manor.
Eanruig, Hal, Hamlin, Hank, Hanraoi, Hark, Harry, Heinrich, Heinrick. Hendrick, Henri, Henrik

Herbert   Teutonic 'Brilliant warrior'.
Bert, Harbert, Harbin, Hebert, Herb, Herbie, Heriberto, Hoireabard

Herrick   Teutonic 'Army ruler'.

Hewett   Anglo-Saxon 'Little Hugh'.

Hezekiah Hebrew 'God is strength'. Belief in God arms this man against all adversity.

Hilary Latin 'Cheerful and merry'.
Hilaire, Hillary, Hillery

Hilton Anglo-Saxon 'From the hill farm'.
Hylton

Hiram Hebrew 'Most noble and exalted one'.
Hi, Hy, Hyram

Hogan Celtic 'Youth'.

Holbrook Anglo-Saxon 'From the brook in the valley'.

Holcomb Anglo-Saxon 'Deep valley'.
Holcombe, Holecomb, Holecombe

Holden Anglo-Saxon/Teutonic 'From the valley' or 'kind'.

Holgate Anglo-Saxon 'Gatekeeper'.

Hollis Anglo-Saxon 'One who lives in the holly grove'.

Holmes Anglo-Saxon 'From the island in the river'.

Holt Anglo-Saxon 'From the forest'.

Homer Greek 'A pledge'.

Horace Latin 'Time keeper' or 'hours of the sun'.
Horatio, Horatius, Race

Houston Anglo-Saxon 'From the town in the mountains'.

Howard Anglo-Saxon 'Chief guardian'.
Howie

Howe Teutonic 'The eminent one'. A person of high birth.

Howell Celtic 'Little, alert one'.
Hywel, Hywell

Hubert Teutonic 'Brilliant, shining mind'.
Aodh, Aoidh, Bert, Hobart, Hobbard, Hoibeard,
Hoireabard, Hoyt, Hubbard, Hube, Huey, Hughes, Hugo

Hudson Anglo-Saxon 'Son of the hoodsman'.

Hugh Teutonic 'Brilliant mind'.
Hewe, Hughie, Hughy

Hulbert Teutonic 'Graceful'.
Hulbard, Hulburd, Hulburt

Humbert Teutonic 'Brilliant Hun' or 'Bright home'.
Bert, Bertie, Berty, Humbie, Umberto

Humphrey Teutonic 'Protector of the peace'.
Humfrey, Humfry, Hump, Humph

Hunter Anglo-Saxon 'A hunter'.
Hunt

Huntingdon Anglo-Saxon 'Hill of the hunter'.

Huntington Anglo-Saxon 'Hunting estate'.

Hurley Gaelic 'Sea tide'.

Hurst Anglo-Saxon 'One who lives in the forest'.
Hearst

Hussein Arabic 'Small and handsome'.

Huxley Anglo-Saxon 'Hugh's meadow'.

Hyatt Anglo-Saxon 'From the high gate'.
Hiatt

Hyde Anglo-Saxon 'From the hide of land'. An old unit of
measurement of land.

boys

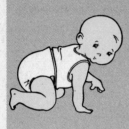

I

Iago Hebrew 'Supplanter'.

Ian Celtic 'God is gracious'.
Iaian, Iain

Ibald Teutonic 'Princely archer'.

Icabod Hebrew 'Departed glory'.

Icarus Greek 'Dedicated to the moon'.

Iden Anglo-Saxon 'Prosperous'.

Idris Welsh 'Fiery lord'.

Idwal Welsh 'Wall lord'.

Ignatius Latin 'The ardent one'. A fiery patriot.
Ignace, Ignacio, Ignate, Ignazio, Inigo

Igor Scandinavian 'The hero'.

Imala Native American 'One who disciplines firmly'.

Imo Hebrew 'Beloved'.

Imran Arabic/Sanskrit 'Host' (Arabic) or 'strong' (Sanskrit).

Indra Hindi 'Raindrop' or 'god-like'.

Ingemar Norse 'Famous son'.
Ingmar

Inger Norse 'A son's army'.
Ingar, Ingvar

Ingram Teutonic 'The raven' or 'the raven's son'.
Ingraham

Ionwyn Welsh 'Fair lord'.

Ira Hebrew 'The watcher'.

Irving Anglo-Saxon/Celtic 'Friend of the sea' (Anglo-Saxon) or 'white river' (Celtic).
Irvin, Irvine, Irwin, Erwin

Isaac Hebrew 'The laughing one'.
Ike, Ikey, Ikie, Isaak, Izaak

Isaiah Hebrew 'God is my helper'.

Isham Anglo-Saxon 'From the estate of the iron man'.

Ishi Hebrew 'Husband'.

Ishmael Hebrew 'The wanderer'.

Israel Hebrew 'The Lord's soldier'. The warrior of God.
Issie, Izzie

Ithnan Hebrew 'The strong sailor'.

Ivar Norse 'Battle archer'. The warrior with the long bow.
Iven, Iver, Ives, Ivo, Ivon, Ivor

Ives Anglo-Saxon 'Son of the archer' or derivative of Ivar.
Yves

Ivor Welsh 'Lord'.
Ifor

Izod Celtic 'Fair'.

Jabez Hebrew 'Cause of sorrow'.

Jacinto Spanish 'Purple flower'.

Jack Hebrew 'God's gracious gift'. A variation of John.

Jackson Old English 'Son of Jack'.

Jacob Hebrew 'The supplanter'.
Cobb, Diego, Hamish, Jacobus, Jacques, Jake, James, Jas, Jem, Jemmie, Jemmy, Jim, Jimmie, Jimmy, Jock, Jocko, Seamus, Seumas, Shamus

Jael Hebrew 'To ascend'.

Jagger Northumbrian 'A carter'.

Jake Hebrew 'The supplanter'. A variation of Jacob.

Jalaad Arabic 'Glory'.

Jaleel Arabic 'Majestic'.

Jamal Arabic 'Beauty'.
Jamaal

James   Hebrew 'The supplanter'. Derivative of Jacob.
Hamish, Jamie, Jock, Seamus, Seumas, Shamus

Jamil   Arabic 'Handsome'.

Jason   Greek 'The healer'.
Jasun

Jay   Anglo-Saxon 'Jay or crow'. Also used as diminutive for any name beginning with J.

Jedediah   Hebrew 'Beloved by the Lord'.
Jed, Jeddy, Jedidiah

Jefferson   Anglo-Saxon 'Jeffrey's son'.

Jehiel   Hebrew 'May God live'.

Jeremy   Hebrew 'Exalted by the Lord'.
Jeramey, Jere, Jeremiah, Jeremias, Jerry

Jerome   Latin 'Sacred, holy'. A man of God.
Gerome, Jerry

Jesse   Hebrew 'God's gift'.
Jess

Jesus   Hebrew 'God will help'.

Jethro   Hebrew 'Excellent, without equal'.

Joachim   Hebrew 'Judgement of the Lord'.
Akim, Joaquin

Job   Hebrew 'The persecuted, the afflicted'.

Jodel   Latin 'Sportive'.

Joel   Hebrew 'The Lord is God'.
Joe, Joey

John Hebrew 'God's gracious gift'.
Eoin, Evan, Geno, Gian, Gianni, Giovanni, Hans, Iaian, Iain, Ian, Ivan, Jack, Jackie, Jan, Janos, Jean, Jevon, Jock, Johan, Johann, Johnnie, Johnny, Jon, Juan, Seain, Sean, Seann, Shane, Shawn, Sian, Siùn, Zane

Jonah Hebrew 'Peace'.

Jonas Hebrew 'Dove'. A man of peace and tranquillity.

Jonathan Hebrew 'Gift of the Lord'.
Jon, Jonathon

Jordan Hebrew 'The descending river'.
Jordon, Jourdain

Joseph Hebrew 'He shall add'.
Isoep, Jodi, Jodu, Joe, Joey, Jose, Josiah, Jozef, Seosaidh

Joshua Hebrew 'God's salvation'. A man saved by his belief in God.
Josh

Jotham Hebrew 'God is perfect'.

Judd Hebrew 'Praised, extolled'.
Judah, Jude

Julius Latin 'Youthful shaveling'.
Joliet, Jolyon, Jule, Jules, Julian

Junius Latin 'Born in June'.

Justin Latin 'The just one'. One of upright principles and morals.
Iestin, Just, Justinian, Justino, Justus

boys

K

Kadmiel	Hebrew 'God is the ancient one'.
Kalil	Arabic 'Good friend'. *Kahaleel*
Kamal	Arabic 'Perfect'.
Kane	Celtic 'Little, war-like one' or 'radiant brightness'. *Kayne*
Kay	Celtic 'Rejoiced in'. Also diminutive for any name beginning with K.
Keane	Anglo-Saxon 'Bold and handsome'. A sharp-witted man.
Kedar	Arabic 'Powerful'.
Keefe	Celtic 'Handsome, noble and admirable'.
Keegan	Celtic 'Little fiery one'.
Keelan	Celtic 'Little slender one'.
Keeley	Celtic 'Little handsome one'.

Keenan Celtic 'Little ancient one'.
Keen, Kienan

Keith Celtic 'A place' or 'from the forest'.

Kelly Gaelic 'The warrior'.
Kellen, Kelley

Kelsey Norse/Teutonic 'One who lives on the island'.

Kelvin Gaelic 'From the narrow stream'.
Kelvan, Kelven, Kelwin

Kemp Anglo-Saxon 'The warrior champion'.

Kendall Celtic 'Chief of the valley'.
Ken, Kendal, Kendell

Kendrick Anglo-Saxon/Gaelic 'Royal ruler, son of Henry'.

Kenn Celtic 'Clear as bright water'.
Kennan, Kenon

Kennard Anglo-Saxon 'Bold and vigorous'.

Kennedy Gaelic 'The helmeted chief'.

Kenneth Celtic 'The handsome' or 'royal oath'.
Ken, Keneth, Kennet, Kennith, Kenny, Kent

Kent Celtic 'Bright and white'. Also diminutive of Kenneth.

Kenton Anglo-Saxon 'From the royal estate'.

Kenyon Celtic 'White haired'.

Kern Gaelic 'Little dark one'.

Kerry Gaelic 'Son of the dark one'.

Kerwin Gaelic 'Small black haired one'.
Kirwin

Kevin   Gaelic 'Gentle, kind and lovable'.
Kev, Kevan, Keven, Kevon

Khalid   Arabic 'Immortal'.

Khalil   Arabic 'Friend'.

Kieran   Gaelic 'Small and dark skinned'.
Kerrin, Kerry, Kiernan, Kieron

Kimball   Celtic 'Royally brave' or 'warrior chief'.
Kembell, Kemble, Kim, Kimbell, Kimble

Kincaid   Celtic 'Battle chief'.

King   Anglo-Saxon 'The sovereign'. The ruler of his people.

Kingsley   Anglo-Saxon 'From the king's meadow'.
Kinsley

Kingston   Anglo-Saxon 'From the king's farm'.

Kingswell   Anglo-Saxon 'From the king's well'.

Kirby   Teutonic 'From the church village'.
Kerby, Kerr

Kirk   Norse 'One who lives at the church'.

Knight   Anglo-Saxon 'Mounted soldier'.

Knox   Anglo-Saxon 'From the hills'.

Krishna   Hindi 'Delightful'.
Krisha

Kyle   Gaelic 'From the strait'.
Kiel

boys

L

Laban	Hebrew 'White'.
Lachlan	Celtic 'War-like'.
Lacy	Latin 'From the Roman manor house'.
Ladd	Anglo-Saxon 'Attendant, page'. *Laddie*
Laird	Celtic 'The land owner'. The lord of the manor.
Lamar	Teutonic 'Famous throughout the land'.
Lambert	Teutonic 'Rich in land'. An owner of vast estates.
Lancelot	French 'Spear attendant'. *Lance, Lancey, Launce, Launcelot*
Landon	Anglo-Saxon 'One who lives on the long hill'. *Langdon, Langston*
Lane	Anglo-Saxon 'From the narrow road'. *Laina, Layne*
Langford	Anglo-Saxon 'One who lives by the long ford'.

Langley Anglo-Saxon 'One who lives by the long meadow'.

Langston Anglo-Saxon 'The farm belonging to the tall man'.
Langsdon

Langworth Anglo-Saxon 'From the long enclosure'.

Latimer Anglo-Saxon 'The interpreter, the language teacher'.

Lawford Anglo-Saxon 'One who lives at the ford by the hill'.

Lawrence Latin 'Crowned with laurels'. The victor's crown of bay leaves.
*Labhras, Labhruinn, Larrance, Larry, Lars, Lauren,
Laurence, Laurent, Lauric, Lauritz, Lawrance, Lawry, Lon,
Lonnie, Loren, Lorenz, Lorenze, Lorenzo, Lori, Lorin,
Lorne, Lorrie, Lorry*

Lawson Anglo-Saxon 'Son of Lawrence'.

Lawton Anglo-Saxon 'From the town on the hill'.
Laughton

Leander Greek 'The lion man'.
Leandro

Lee Anglo-Saxon/Gaelic 'From the meadow' (Anglo-Saxon) or
'poetic' (Gaelic).
Leigh

Leif Norse 'The beloved one'.

Leighton Anglo-Saxon 'One who lives at the farm by the meadow'.
Layton

Leith Celtic 'Broad, wide river'.

Leland Anglo-Saxon 'One who lives by the meadow land'.
Lealand, Leyland

Lemuel Hebrew 'Consecrated to God'.
Lem, Lemmie

Lennon Gaelic 'Little cloak'.

Lennox Celtic 'Grove of elm trees'.

Leo Latin 'Lion'.

Leon French 'Lion-like'.

Leonard Latin 'Lion brave'. One with all the courage and tenacity of the king of beasts.
Len, Lenard, Lennard, Lennie, Lenny, Leoner, Leonardo, Leonhard, Leonid, Leonidas, Lonnard

Leopold Teutonic 'Brave for the people'. One who fights for his countryman.
Leo, Lepp

Leroy French 'The king'.
Lee, Leroi, Roy

Leslie Celtic 'From the grey fort'.
Les, Lesley

Lester Anglo-Saxon 'From the army camp'.
Leicester

Levi Hebrew 'United'.
Levin

Lewis Teutonic 'Famous battle warrior'.
Clovis, Lew, Lewes, Lou, Louis, Ludo, Ludovic, Ludovick, Ludwig, Lugaidh, Luigi, Luis, Luthais

Liam Celtic 'Determined protector'. Variation of William.

Lind Anglo-Saxon 'From the lime tree'.
Linden, Lindon, Lyndon

Lindley Anglo-Saxon 'By the lime tree in the meadow'.

Lindsey Anglo-Saxon 'Pool island'.
Lind, Lindsay. Linsay, Linsey

Linford Anglo-Saxon 'From the lime tree ford'.

Linus Greek 'Flax-coloured hair'.

Lionel French 'The young lion'.
Lion, Lionello

Litton Anglo-Saxon 'Farm on the hillside'.

Llewellyn Welsh 'Lion-like' or 'like a ruler'.

Lloyd Welsh 'Grey haired'.
Floyd

Logan Celtic 'Little hollow'.

London Middle English 'Fortress of the moon'.

Lorimer Latin 'Harness maker'.

Lowell Anglo-Saxon 'The beloved one'.
Lovel, Lovell, Lowe

Lucius Latin 'Light'.
Luc, Lucais, Lucas, Luce, Lucian, Lucio, Luck, Lukas, Luke, Lukey

Luke Latin 'Light'. Also variation of Lucius.

Luther Teutonic 'Famous warrior'.
Lothaire, Lothar, Lothario, Lute

Lyle French 'From the island'.
Liall, Lisle, Lyall, Lyell

Lyman Anglo-Saxon 'Man from the meadow'.
Leyman

Lynn Welsh 'From the pool or waterfall'.
Lin, Linn, Lyn

Lysander Greek 'The liberator'.
Sandy

Mabon Welsh 'Youth'.

Mac Celtic Used in many Scots and Irish names and meaning Son of. Also used in the form 'Mc'. For instance Macadam (Son of Adam), McDonald (Son of Donald) and so on.

Macy French 'From Matthew's estate'.

Maddock Welsh 'Beneficent'.
Maddox, Madoc, Madock, Madog

Madison Anglo-Saxon 'Mighty in battle'.
Maddison

Magnus Latin 'The great one'. One who excels all others.

Maitland Anglo-Saxon 'One who lives in the meadow land'.

Major Latin 'Greater'. Anything you can do, he can do better!

Malcolm Celtic 'The dove' or 'follower of St Columba'.

Malik Muslim 'Master'.

Malin Anglo-Saxon 'Little warrior'.

Mallory   Anglo-Saxon/Latin 'Army counsellor (Anglo-Saxon) or 'unlucky' (Latin).
Malory

Maloney   Gaelic 'Believer in the Sabbath'.

Malvin   Celtic 'Polished chief'.
Mal, Mel, Melvin

Manfred   Anglo-Saxon 'Peaceful hero'.
Manfried

Manley   Anglo-Saxon 'The hero's meadow'.
Manleich

Manning   Anglo-Saxon 'Hero's son'.

Mansfield   Anglo-Saxon 'Hero's field'.

Manville   French 'From the great estate'.
Manvil

Marcel   Latin 'Little follower of Mars'. A war-like person.
Marcello, Marcellus

Marion   French 'Bitter'. A French form of Mary, often given as a boy's name in compliment to the Virgin.

Marius   Latin 'The martial one'.
Mario

Mark   Latin 'Follower of Mars, the warrior'.
Marc, Marco, Marcus

Marland   Anglo-Saxon 'One who lives in the lake land'.

Marlow   Anglo-Saxon 'From the lake on the hill'.
Marlowe

Marmaduke   Celtic 'Sea leader'.
Duke

Marsden Anglo-Saxon 'From the marshy valley'.
Marsdon

Marsh Anglo-Saxon 'From the marsh'.

Marshall Anglo-Saxon 'The steward'. The man who looked after the estate of a nobleman.

Marston Anglo-Saxon 'From the farm by the lake'.

Martin Latin 'War-like person'. A follower of Mars.
Mart, Martainn, Marten, Martie, Martino, Marton, Marty

Marvin Anglo-Saxon 'Famous friend'.
Marwin, Mervin, Merwin, Merwyn

Marwood Anglo-Saxon 'From the lake in the forest'.

Maslin French 'Small Thomas'.
Maslen, Maslon

Mason Latin 'Worker in stone'.

Massey English 'Twin'.

Math Welsh 'Treasure'.

Mather Anglo-Saxon 'Powerful army'.

Matmon Hebrew 'Treasure'.

Matthew Hebrew 'Gift of God'. One of the 12 apostles.
Mat, Mata, Mathew, Mathias, Matt, Mattie, Matty, Matthias, Mattias

Maurice Latin 'Moorish-looking, dark-complexioned'.
Maury, Maurey, Mauricio, Maurizio, Mo, Morel, Morice, Moritz, Morrell, Morrie, Morris, Morry

Max Popular variation of Maximilian or Maxwell.

Maximilian Latin 'The greatest, the most excellent'. One without equal.
Max, Maxey, Maxie, Maxim, Maximilien, Maxy

Maxwell   Anglo-Saxon 'Large spring of fresh water'.
Max, Maxi, Maxie

Mayer   Latin 'Greater'.
Myer

Mayfield   Anglo-Saxon 'From the field of the warrior'.

Maynard   Teutonic 'Powerfully strong and brave'.
Menard

Mead   Anglo-Saxon 'From the meadow'.

Medwin   Teutonic 'Strong and powerful friend'.

Megha   Sanskrit 'Star'.

Meilyr   Welsh 'Man of iron'.

Melbourne   Anglo-Saxon 'From the mill stream'.
Melburn, Melburne, Milbourn, Milbourne, Milburn, Milburne, Pierrot

Melchior   Persian 'King of light'.

Melville   French 'From the estate of the industrious'.
Mel, Melvil

Mendel   Semitic 'Wisdom'.

Mercer   Anglo-Saxon 'Merchant'.

Meredith   Welsh 'Guardian from the sea'.
Meredydd, Meredyth, Merideth, Meridith, Meridyth, Merry

Merle   Latin 'The blackbird' or 'the black haired one'.

Merlin   Anglo-Saxon 'The falcon'. The legendary wizard of King Arthur's court.
Marl, Marlin, Marlen, Marlon, Merl

Meron   Hebrew 'Army'.

Merrill French 'Little famous one'.
Merritt

Merton Anglo-Saxon 'From the farm by the sea'.

Meryll French from Old German 'King'.

Methuselah Hebrew 'Man of the javelin'.

Meven Celtic/French 'Agile'.

Michael Hebrew 'Like the Lord'.
Micah, Mich, Michel, Mickie, Micky, Mike, Mischa, Mitch, Mitchell, Mithell

Milan Slavic 'Beloved'.

Milburn Old English 'Mill stream'.

Miles Greek/Latin 'The soldier'.
Myles

Milford Anglo-Saxon 'From the mill ford'.
Millford

Millard French 'Strong and victorious'.

Miller Anglo-Saxon 'Grain grinder'.

Milo Latin 'The miller'.
Mylo

Milton Anglo-Saxon 'From the mill town'.
Milt

Milward Anglo-Saxon 'The mill keeper'.

Miroslav Slavonic 'Peace, glory'.

Modred Anglo-Saxon 'Brave counsellor'. One who advised honestly without fear of reprisal.

Mohamad	Sanskrit 'Prophet of Islam'. *Mohammed*
Mohammed	Arabic/Sanskrit 'Praised'. *Muhammad*
Monroe	Celtic 'From the red swamp'. *Monro, Munro, Munroe*
Montague	French 'From the jagged mountain'. *Montagu, Monte, Monty*
Montgomery	French 'The mountain hunter'. *Monte, Monty*
Moore	French 'Dark complexioned, Moor'. *More*
Mordecai	Hebrew 'Belonging to Marduk'. *Mort*
Moreland	Anglo-Saxon 'From the moors'.
Morgan	Welsh 'White sea'. The foam flecked waves. *Morganica, Morganne, Morgen*
Morrell	Latin 'Dark'.
Morrison	Anglo-Saxon 'Maurice's son'. *Morison*
Morse	Anglo-Saxon 'Maurice's son'.
Mortimer	French 'From the quiet water'. *Mortemer, Mortermer, Morthermer*
Morton	Anglo-Saxon 'From the farm on the moor'. *Morten*
Morven	Gaelic 'Blond giant'. *Morfin*

Moses Hebrew 'Saved from the water'. The great prophet of Israel.
Moe, Moise, Mose, Mosie, Moss

Moustapha Arabic 'Chosen'.
Mustapha

Mubarak Arabic 'Blessed'.

Muir Celtic 'From the moor'.

Mungo Gaelic 'Lovable'.

Murad Arabic 'Desired' or 'wanted'.

Murdoch Celtic 'Prosperous from the sea'.
Murdock, Murtagh

Murphy Gaelic 'Sea warrior'.

Murray Celtic 'The mariner' or 'sea fighter'.

Myron Greek 'The fragrant oil'.
Merrill

Nadim Arabic 'Repentant'.

Nadir Arabic/Sanskrit 'Rare, precious, the pinnacle'.

Nairn Celtic 'One who lives by the alder tree'.

Namir Hebrew 'Leopard'.

Napoleon Greek 'Lion of the woodland dell'.

Nash Old French 'Cliff'.

Nathan Hebrew 'Gift of God'.
Nat, Nataniel, Nate, Nathaniel, Nattie

Neal Gaelic 'The champion'.
Neale, Neall, Neel, Neil, Neill, Niall, Niels, Niles, Nils

Nelson Celtic 'Son of Neal'.
Nils, Nilson

Nero Latin 'Dark complexioned, black haired'.
Neron

Nestor Greek 'Ancient wisdom'.

Neville Latin 'From the new town'.
Nev, Nevil, Nevile

Nevin Gaelic/Anglo-Saxon 'Worshipper of saints' (Gaelic) or 'nephew' (Anglo-Saxon).
Nefen, Nevins, Niven, Nivens

Newell Anglo-Saxon 'From the new hall'.
Newall

Newland Anglo-Saxon 'From the new lands'.
Newlands

Newlin Celtic 'One who lives by the new pool'.
Newlyn

Newman Anglo-Saxon 'The newcomer, the new arrival'.

Newton Anglo-Saxon 'From the new estate'.

Nicholas Greek 'Victorious people's army'. The leader of the people.
Claus, Cole, Colin, Colley, Klaus, Neacail, Niccolo, Nichol, Nicholl, Nick, Nickie, Nicky, Nicol, Nicolai, Nicolas, Nik, Nikki, Nikos, Niles

Nigel Latin 'Black haired one'.

Nixon Anglo-Saxon 'Nicholas's son'.
Nickson

Noah Hebrew 'Rest, comfort and peace'.
Noach

Noble Latin 'Noble and famous'.
Nobel, Nolan, Noland

Noel French 'Born at Christmas'. A suitable name for a boy born on Christmas Day.
Natal, Natale, Newel, Newell, Nowell

Nolan Celtic 'Famous'.

Norbert Teutonic 'Brilliant sea hero'. The courageous commander of ships'.
Norbie

Norman French 'Man from the north, a Northman'. The bold Viking from Scandinavia.
Norm, Normand, Normie, Norris

Northcliffe Anglo-Saxon 'Man from the north cliff'.
Northcliff

Northrop Anglo-Saxon 'From the northern farm'.
North, Northrup, Nortrop, Nortrup

Norton Anglo-Saxon 'From the north farm'.

Norville French 'From the north town'.
Norvel, Norvie, Norvil

Norward Anglo-Saxon 'Guardian from the north'.

Norwell Anglo-Saxon 'From the north well'.

Norwood Anglo-Saxon 'From the north forest'.

Oakes   Anglo-Saxon 'One who lives by the oak tree'.

Oakley   Anglo-Saxon 'From the oak tree meadow'.
Okely

Obadiah   Hebrew 'Servant of the Lord'. The obedient one.
Obadias

Obert   Teutonic 'Wealthy and brilliant'.

Octavius   Latin 'The eighth born'.
Octavian, Octave, Octavus, Tavey

Odell   Teutonic 'Wealthy one'.
Odie, Odin, Odo

Odolf   Teutonic 'The wealthy wolf'.

Ogden   Anglo-Saxon 'From the oak valley'.
Ogdan

Ogilvie   Celtic 'From the high peak'.

Olaf Scandinavian 'Ancestral relic' or 'peaceful reminder'.
Amhlaoibh, Olav, Olen, Olin

<u>**Oliver**</u> Latin 'Symbol of peace'. The olive branch.
Noll, Nollie, Nolly, Olivero, Oliviero, Ollie, Olvan

Olney Anglo-Saxon 'Olla's island'.

Oman Scandinavian 'High protector'.

Omar Arabic/Sanskrit 'The first son' or 'most high follower of the prophet'.

Onslow Anglo-Saxon 'Hill of the zealous one'.

Oram Anglo-Saxon 'From the enclosure by the riverbank'.

Oran Gaelic 'Pale-skinned man'.
Oren, Orin, Orran, Orren, Orrin

Orford Anglo-Saxon 'One who lives at the cattle ford'.

Orion Greek 'The son of light'.

Ormond Teutonic 'Spearman' or 'shipman'.
Orman, Ormand, Ormen, Ormin

Oro Spanish 'Golden-haired one'.

Orrick Anglo-Saxon 'One who lives by the ancient oak tree'.

Orson Anglo-Saxon/Latin 'Son of the spearman' (Anglo-Saxon) or 'little bear' (Latin).
Urson

Orton Anglo-Saxon 'From the shore-farmstead'.

Orval Anglo-Saxon 'Mighty with a spear'.

Orville French 'From the golden town'.
Orvil

Orvin Anglo-Saxon 'Spear friend'.

Osbert Anglo-Saxon 'Divinely bright warrior'.
Bert, Bertie, Berty, Oz, Ozzie

Osborn Anglo-Saxon 'Divine warrior'.
Osborne, Osbourn, Osbourne, Osburn, Osburne

Oscar Anglo-Saxon 'Divine spearman'. A fighter for God.
Os, Oskar, Ossie, Oz, Ozzie

Osgood Scandinavian 'The divine Goth'.

Osmond Anglo-Saxon 'Divine protector'.

Oswald Anglo-Saxon 'Divinely powerful'.

Otis Greek 'Keen of sight and hearing'.
Oates

Otto Teutonic 'Wealthy, prosperous man'.
Otho

Otway Teutonic 'Fortunate in battle'.

Owen Celtic 'The young, well-born warrior'.
Owain

Oxford Anglo-Saxon 'From the ford where oxen crossed'.

Padgett French 'The young attendant, a page'.
Padget, Page, Paget, Paige

Paine Latin 'The country rustic, a pagan'.
Payne

Palladin Native American 'Fighter'.

Palmer Latin 'The palm-bearing pilgrim'.
Palm

Park Anglo-Saxon 'From the park'.
Parke

Parker Anglo-Saxon 'The park keeper'. One who guarded the park lands.

Parkin Anglo-Saxon 'Little Peter'.
Perkin, Peterkin

Parr Anglo-Saxon 'One who lives by the cattle pen'.

Parrish Anglo-Saxon 'From the church parish'.
Parish

Parry French/Celtic 'Protector'.

Pascal Italian 'Easter born'. The new-born pascal lamb.
Pasquale

Patrick Latin 'The noble patrician'. One of noble birth and from a noble line.
Paddy, Padraic, Padraig, Padruig, Pat, Patric, Patrice, Patricio, Patrizio, Patrizius, Patsy, Peyton, Rick

Patton Anglo-Saxon 'From the warrior's farm'.
Patin

Paul Latin 'Little'.
Pablo, Paley, Paolo, Pauley, Paulie, Pavel

Paxton Anglo-Saxon 'From the warrior's estate'.

Payton Anglo-Saxon 'One who lives on the warrior's farm'.
Peyton

Pelton Anglo-Saxon 'From the farm by the pool'.

Pembroke Celtic 'From the headland'.

Penn Anglo-Saxon 'Enclosure'.

Percival French 'Valley piercer'.
Parsefal, Parsifal, Perc, Perce, Perceval, Percy, Purcell

Peregrine Latin 'The wanderer'.
Perry

Perry Anglo-Saxon 'From the pear tree'. Also diminutive of *Peregrine*

Perth Celtic 'Thorn bush thicket'.

Peter Latin 'The stone, the rock'. The first pope.
Parnell, Peadar, Pearce, Pedro, Pernell, Perrin, Pete, Petrie, Pierce, Piero, Pierre, Pierro, Pierrot, Piers, Pietro

Phelps   Anglo-Saxon 'Son of Philip'.

Philemon   Greek 'Kiss'.

<u>Philip</u>   Greek 'Lover of horses'.
Filib, Filip, Filli, Phelps, Philipp, Phillip, Phillopa, Pilib, Phill, Phillie, Philly

Phillips   Anglo-Saxon 'Phillip's son'.
Felips, Fellips, Phelips, Phellips, Phellipps, Philips, Phillipps

Philo   Greek 'Friendly love'.

Phineas   Greek 'Mouth of brass'.

Pickford   Anglo-Saxon 'From the ford at the peak'.

Pickworth   Anglo-Saxon 'From the estate of the hewer'.

Pitney   Dutch from Teutonic 'Preserving one's island'.

Pitt   Anglo-Saxon 'From the hollow'.

Plato   Greek 'The broad shouldered one'. The great philosopher.

Platt   French 'From the plateau'.

Po Sin   Chinese 'Grandfather elephant'.

Pollock   Anglo-Saxon 'Little Paul'.

Porter   French 'Gatekeeper'.

Powell   Celtic 'Alert' or 'Son of Howell'.

Prentice   Anglo-Saxon 'A learner or apprentice'.
Prentiss

Prescott   Anglo-Saxon 'From the priest's house'.
Prescot

Preston   Anglo-Saxon 'From the priest's farm'.

Price   Celtic 'Son of a loving man'.

Primo Latin 'The first born son'.

Prince Latin 'Chief'.

Prior Latin 'The Father Superior, the Head of the Monastery'.
Pryor

Prosper Latin 'Fortunate'.

Putnam Anglo-Saxon 'From the pit estate'.

Qabil   Arabic 'Able'.

Qadir   Arabic 'Powerful'.

Quentin   Latin 'The fifth born'.
Quent, Quinton, Quintin, Quintus

Quigley   Gaelic 'Distaff'.

Quillan   Gaelic 'Cub'.

Quimby   Norse 'From the woman's estate'.
Quemby, Quenby, Quinby

Quincy   French/Latin 'From the fifth son's estate'.

Quinlan   Gaelic 'The well formed one'. One with the body of an Adonis.

Quinn   Gaelic 'Wise and intelligent'.

boys

Radborne Anglo-Saxon 'From the red stream'.
Radbourn, Radbourne, Redbourn, Redbourne

Radcliffe Anglo-Saxon 'From the red cliff'.
Radcliff, Redcliff, Redcliffe

Radford Anglo-Saxon 'From the red ford'.
Radvers, Redford, Redvers

Radley Anglo-Saxon 'From the red meadow'.
Radleigh, Redley, Ridley

Radnor Anglo-Saxon 'From the red shore'.

Radolf Anglo-Saxon 'Wolf counsellor'. Wolf is used in the sense 'brave man'.

Rafferty Gaelic 'Prosperous and rich'.

Ragmar Teutonic 'Wise warrior'.

Raleigh Anglo-Saxon 'One who lives in the meadow of the roe deer'.
Ralegh, Rawleigh, Rawley

R
boys

Ralph Anglo-Saxon 'Counsel wolf'.
Raff, Ralf, Raoul, Raul, Rolf, Rolph

Ralston Anglo-Saxon 'One who lives on Ralph's farm'.

Rama Sanskrit 'Bringer of joy'.

Rambert Teutonic 'Brilliant and mighty'.

Ramiro Spanish 'Great judge'.

Ramsden Anglo-Saxon 'Ram's valley'.

Ramsey Anglo-Saxon 'From Ram's island' or 'from the raven's island'.

Rana Sanskrit 'Prince'.

Rance African 'Borrowed all'.
Ransell

Randal Old English 'Shield wolf'.
Rand, Randall, Randolf, Randolph, Ranulf

Ranger French 'Keeper of the forest'. The gamekeeper who looked after the trees and the wildlife.

Rankin Anglo-Saxon 'Little shield'.

Ransford Anglo-Saxon 'From the raven's ford'.

Ransley Anglo-Saxon 'From the raven's meadow'.

Ransom Anglo-Saxon 'Shield warrior's son.

Raphael Hebrew 'Healed by God'.
Rafael, Rafaello, Rafe, Raff, Raffaello

Rawson Anglo-Saxon 'Son of the little wolf'.

Ray French 'The sovereign'. Also diminutive of Raymond.

Raymond Teutonic 'Wise protection'.
Raimond, Ramon, Ray, Raymon, Raymund, Reamonn

Raynor Scandinavian 'Mighty army'.
Rainer, Rainier

Redman Anglo-Saxon 'Counsellor, advice giver'.

Redmond Anglo-Saxon 'Counsellor, protector, advisor'.
Radmund, Redmund

Redwald Anglo-Saxon 'Mighty counsellor'.

Reece Celtic 'The ardent one'. One who loves living.
Rhett

Reeve Anglo-Saxon 'The steward'. One who looked after a great lord's affairs.

Reginald Teutonic 'Mighty and powerful ruler'.
Naldo, Raghnall, Raynold, Reg, Reggie, Reggy, Reinhold, Renaldo, Renato, Renaud, Renault, Rene, Reynold, Rinaldo, Ron, Ronald, Ronnie, Ronny

Reinhart Teutonic 'Incorruptible'.

Remington Anglo-Saxon 'From the farm where the blackbirds sing'.

Rene Gaelic 'Mighty and powerful'.

Renfrew Celtic 'From the still river'.

Renshaw Anglo-Saxon 'From the forest of the ravens'.

Renton Anglo-Saxon 'From the farm of the roe buck'.

Reuben Hebrew 'Behold a son'.
Rube, Ruben, Rubey, Ruby

Rex Latin 'The king'. The all-powerful monarch.
Rey, Roy

Reyhan   Arabic 'Favoured of God'.

Reynard   Teutonic 'Mighty courage' or 'the fox'.
Raynard, Rehard, Reinhard, Renaud, Rennard

Rezon   Hebrew 'Prince'.

Rhodes   Greek 'The place of roses'.

Rhys   Celtic 'Hero'.
Reece, Rees

Richard   Teutonic 'Wealthy, powerful one'.
*Diccon, Dick, Dickie, Dickon, Dicky, Ricard, Ricardo, Rich,
Richerd, Rick, Rickert, Rickie, Ricky, Riocard, Ritch, Ritchie*

Richmond   Anglo-Saxon 'Powerful protector'.
Richman

Ridgley   Anglo-Saxon 'From the ridge meadow'.

Ridpath   Anglo-Saxon 'From the red path'.
Redpath

Rigby   Anglo-Saxon 'Valley of the ruler'.

Rigg   Anglo-Saxon 'From the ridge'.

Riley   Gaelic 'Valiant and war-like'.
Reilly, Ryley

Riordan   Gaelic 'Royal bard'.
Rearden, Reardon

Ripley   Anglo-Saxon 'From the valley of the echo'.

Risley   Anglo-Saxon 'From the brushwood meadow'.

Ritter   Teutonic 'A knight'.

Roald   Teutonic 'Famous ruler'.

R
boys

Roan Anglo-Saxon 'From the rowan tree'.
Rowan

Roarke Gaelic 'Famous ruler'.
Rorke, Rourke, Ruark

Robert Teutonic 'Bright, shining fame'. A man of brilliant reputation.
Bob, Bobbie, Bobby, Rab, Rabbie, Rabby, Rob, Robbie, Robby, Roberto, Robin, Rupert, Ruprecht

Robinson Anglo-Saxon 'Son of Robert'.

Rochester Anglo-Saxon 'Camp on the rocks'.

Rock Anglo-Saxon 'From the rock'.
Roc, Rocky

Rockley Anglo-Saxon 'From the rocky meadow'.
Rockly

Rockwell Anglo-Saxon 'From the rocky well'.

Roderick Teutonic 'Famous wealthy ruler'.
Broderic, Broderick, Brodrick, Rick, Rickie, Ricky, Rod, Rodd, Roddie, Roddy, Roderic, Roderigo, Rodric, Rodrick, Rory, Rurik

Rodman Teutonic 'Famous hero'.
Rodmond, Rodmund

Rodney Teutonic 'Famous and renowned'.
Rod, Roddie, Roddy, Rodi

Rogan Gaelic 'The red-haired one'.

Roger Teutonic 'Famous spearman; renowned warrior'.
Rodge, Rodger, Rog, Rogerio

Roland Teutonic 'From the famed land'.
Orlando, Rodhlann, Roley, Rollin, Rollo, Rowe, Rowland

Rolt Teutonic 'Power and fame'.

Romeo Latin 'Man from Rome'.

Romero Latin 'Wanderer'.

Romney Celtic 'Curving river'.

Ronan Gaelic 'Little seal'.

Ronson Anglo-Saxon 'Son of Ronald'.

Rooney Gaelic 'The red one'. One with a ruddy complexion.
Rowney, Ruan

Rory Gaelic 'Red king'. Also derivative of Roderick.
Rorie, Rorry, Ruaidhri

Roscoe Scandinavian 'From the deer forest'.
Ros, Rosco, Roz

Roslin French 'Small red-haired one'.
Roslyn, Rosselin, Rosslyn

Ross Celtic/Teutonic 'From the peninsula' (Celtic) or 'horse' (Teutonic).

Roswald Teutonic 'Mighty steed'.
Roswall, Roswell

Rothwell Norse 'From the red well'.

Rover Anglo-Saxon 'A wanderer'.

Rowan Gaelic 'Red haired'.
Rowe, Rowen

Rowell Anglo-Saxon 'From the deer well'.

Rowley Anglo-Saxon 'From the rough meadow'.

Rowsan Anglo-Saxon 'Rowan's son'. Son of a red-haired man.

Roxbury Anglo-Saxon 'From the fortress of the rock'.

Roy Celtic 'Red haired' or 'the king'.

Royce Anglo-Saxon 'Son of the king'.

Royd Norse 'From the forest clearing'.

Roydon Norse 'One who lives on the rye hill'.

Rudd Anglo-Saxon 'Ruddy complexion'.

Rudolph Teutonic 'Famous wolf'.
Dolf, Dolph, Rodolf, Rodolph, Rolf, Rolfe, Rollo, Rolph, Rudolf, Rudy

Rudyard Anglo-Saxon 'From the red enclosure'.

Ruskin Teutonic 'Small red-haired one'.

Russell Anglo-Saxon 'Red as a fox'.
Rus, Russ, Russel, Rusty

Rutherford Anglo-Saxon 'From the cattle ford'.

Rutland Norse 'From the stump land'.

Rutledge Anglo-Saxon 'From the red pool'.
Routledge

Ryan Gaelic 'Small king'.

Rylan Anglo-Saxon 'From the rye land'.
Ryland

Ryman Anglo-Saxon 'The rye-seller'.

Ryton Anglo-Saxon 'From the rye farm'.

S

Saadi	Persian 'Wise'.
Sabas	Hebrew 'Rest'.
Saber	French 'A sword'.
Sabin	Latin 'Man from the Sabines'.
Sadoc	Hebrew 'Sacred'.
Sahale	Native American 'Above'.
Sakima	Native American 'King'.
Saladin	Arabic 'Goodness of the faith'.
Salim	Arabic 'Safe, healthy, peace'.
Salisbury	Old English 'Fortified stronghold'.
Salman	Arabic 'Safe' or 'unharmed'.
Salvador	Latin 'The saviour'. *Salvadore, Salvator, Salvatore, Salvidor*
Samir	Arabic 'Entertaining companion'.

Sampson Hebrew 'Sun's man'.
Sam, Sammy, Samson, Sansom, Sim, Simpson, Simson

Samuel Hebrew 'His name is God'.
Sam, Sammie, Sammy

Sanchia Spanish 'Holy'.

Sanders Anglo-Saxon 'Son of Alexander'.
Sanderson, Sandie, Sandy, Saunders, Saunderson

Sanford Anglo-Saxon 'From the sandy ford'.

Sanjay Sanskrit 'Triumphant'.

Sargent Latin 'A military attendant'.
Sarge, Sargie, Serge, Sergeant, Sergent, Sergio

Saul Hebrew 'Called by God'.

Savero Arabic 'Bright'.

Saville French 'The willow estate'.
Savile

Saxon Anglo-Saxon 'People of the swords'.
Saxe

Sayer Celtic 'Carpenter'.
Sayers, Sayre, Sayres

Scanlon Gaelic 'A snarer of hearts'.

Scott Celtic/Latin 'Tattooed warrior (Celtic) or 'from Scotland' (Latin).
Scot, Scottie, Scotty

Scoville French 'From the Scottish estate'.

Scully Gaelic 'Town crier'. The bringer of news in the days before mass media.

Seabrook Anglo-Saxon 'From a brook by the sea'.
Sebrook

Searle Teutonic 'Armed warrior'.
Searl

Seaton French 'From the Say's farm'.
Seeton, Seetin, Seton

Sebastian Latin 'Reverenced one'. An august person.
Seb, Sebastiano, Sebastien

Sedgwick Anglo-Saxon 'From the sword grass place'.

Seeley Anglo-Saxon 'Happy and blessed'.
Sealey, Seely

Selby Teutonic 'From the manor farm'.

Selden Anglo-Saxon 'From the valley of the willow tree'.

Selvac Celtic 'Rich in cattle'.

Selwyn Teutonic 'Friend at the manor house'.
Selwin

Sennett French 'Old and wise'. The all-knowing seer.

Septimus Latin 'Seventh born son'.

Serge French 'Servant'.

Serle Teutonic 'Bearer of arms and weapons'.

Seth Hebrew 'Appointed by God'.

Seton Anglo-Saxon 'From the farm by the sea'.

Severn Anglo-Saxon 'The boundary'.

Seward Anglo-Saxon 'The sea defender'.

Sexton Anglo-Saxon 'Sacristan'. A church official.

Sextus	Latin 'Sixth born son'.
Seymour	Anglo-Saxon/French 'From the moor by the sea'.
Shadwell	Anglo-Saxon 'From the well in the arbour'.
Shalom	Hebrew 'Peace'. *Sholom*
Shanahan	Gaelic 'The wise one'.
Shandy	Anglo-Saxon 'Little boisterous one'.
Shanley	Gaelic 'The venerable hero'.
Shannon	Gaelic 'Old wise one'. *Shanan*
Sharif	Arabic 'Eminent' or 'honourable'.
Shaw	Anglo-Saxon 'From the grove'.
Sheean	Celtic 'Polite, courteous'.
Sheffield	Anglo-Saxon 'From the crooked field'.
Shelby	Anglo-Saxon 'From the estate on the cliff edge'.
Sheldon	Anglo-Saxon 'From the hill ledge'.
Shelley	Anglo-Saxon 'From the meadow on the hill ledge'.
Shelton	Anglo-Saxon 'From the farm on the hill ledge'.
Sherborne	Anglo-Saxon 'From the clear stream'. *Sherbourn, Sherbourne, Sherburn, Sherburne*
Sheridan	Gaelic 'Wild savage'.
Sherwin	Anglo-Saxon 'Loyal friend' or 'swift footed'. *Sherwynd*
Sherwood	Anglo-Saxon 'Bright forest'.

Shipley Anglo-Saxon 'From the sheep meadow'.

Siddell Anglo-Saxon 'From a wide valley'.

Sidney French 'A follower of St. Denis' or 'Man from Sidon'.
Sid, Syd, Sydney

Sigmund Teutonic 'Victorious protector'.
Sigismond, Sigismund, Sigmond

Silas Latin 'From the forest'.
Si, Silvan, Silvano, Silvanus, Silvester, Sly, Sylvan, Sylvester

Simon Hebrew 'One who hears'.
Sim, Simeon, Siomonn, Ximenes

Sinclair French 'From St Clair' or 'shining light'.
St. Clair

Skelly Gaelic 'Historian'.

Skelton Anglo-Saxon 'From the farm on the hill ledge'.

Skip Scandinavian 'Owner of the ship'.
Skipp, Skippy

Skipton Anglo-Saxon 'From the sheep farm'.

Slade Anglo-Saxon 'Valley dweller'.

Slevin Gaelic 'The mountain climber'.
Slaven, Slavin, Sleven

Sloan Gaelic 'Warrior'.
Sloane

Smedley Anglo-Saxon 'From the flat meadow'.
Smedly

Smith Anglo-Saxon 'The blacksmith'.

Snowden Anglo-Saxon 'From the snowy hill'. Man from the snowcapped mountains.

Socrates Greek 'Self-restrained'.

Sol Latin 'The sun'. Also diminutive of Solomon.

Solomon Hebrew 'Wise and peaceful'.
Salomon, Sol, Solamon, Sollie, Solly, Soloman

Solon Greek 'Wise man'. Greek form of Solomon.

Somerset Anglo-Saxon 'From the summer place'. The place where wanderers rested for the summer.

Somerton Anglo-Saxon 'From the summer farm'.

Somerville Anglo-Saxon 'From the summer estate'.
Sommerville

Sorrel French 'With brownish hair'.

Southwell Anglo-Saxon 'From the south well'.

Spalding Anglo-Saxon 'From the split meadow'.
Spaulding

Spangler Teutonic 'The tinsmith'.

Spark Anglo-Saxon 'Gay gallant'. The man about town'.

Speed Anglo-Saxon 'Success, prosperity'.

Spencer French 'Shopkeeper, dispenser of provisions'.
Spence, Spenser

Sproule Anglo-Saxon 'Energetic, active person'.
Sprowle

Squire Anglo-Saxon 'Knight's shield bearer'.

St John English A contraction of St. John.

Stacey   Latin 'Prosperous and stable'.
Stacy

Stafford   Anglo-Saxon 'From the ford by the landing place'.
Staffard

Stamford   Anglo-Saxon 'From the stony crossing'.
Stanford

Standish   Anglo-Saxon 'From the stony park'.

Stanfield   Anglo-Saxon 'From the stony field'.

Stanley   Anglo-Saxon/Slavic 'From the stony meadow' (Anglo-Saxon)
or 'pride of the camp' (Slavic).
Stan, Stanleigh, Stanly

Stanton   Anglo-Saxon 'From the rocky lake' or 'from the stony farm'.

Stanwood   Anglo-Saxon 'From the stony forest'.

Starr   Anglo-Saxon 'A star'.

Staton   Teutonic 'One who lives in the stone house'.

Stavros   Greek 'Cross'.

Stedman   Anglo-Saxon 'Farm owner'. One who owns the land he tills.

Stephen   Greek 'The crowned one'. A man who wears the victor's
laurel wreath.
*Etienne, Stefan, Steffen, Stephanus, Stephenson, Steve,
Steven, Stevenson, Stevie*

Sterling   Teutonic 'Good honest, worthy'.
Stirling

Sterne   Anglo-Saxon 'The austere one, an ascetic'.
Stearn, Stearne, Stern

Stewart Anglo-Saxon 'The steward'. Name of the Royal House of Scotland.
Stew, Steward, Stu, Stuart

Stillman Anglo-Saxon 'Quiet and gentle man'.
Stilman

Stinson Anglo-Saxon 'Son of stone'.

Stockley Anglo-Saxon 'From the cleared meadow'.

Stockton Anglo-Saxon 'From the farm in the clearing'.

Stockwell Anglo-Saxon 'From the well in the clearing'.

Stoddard Anglo-Saxon 'The horse keeper'.

Storm Anglo-Saxon 'The tempest'.

Storr Scandinavian 'Great man'.

Stowe Anglo-Saxon 'From the place'.

Strahan Gaelic 'The poet'.

Stratford Anglo-Saxon 'The street crossing the ford'.

Stroud Anglo-Saxon 'From the thicket'.

Sullivan Gaelic 'Man with black eyes'.
Sullie, Sully

Sumner Latin 'One who summons'. The church official who summoned the congregation to prayer.

Sunil Sanskrit 'Very dark blue'.

Surinder Hindi 'Mightiest of the gods'.

Sutcliffe Anglo-Saxon 'From the south cliff'.
Sutcliff

Sutherland Scandinavian 'From a southern land'.

Sutton   Anglo-Saxon 'From the south town'.

Sweeney   Gaelic 'Little hero'.

Swinton   Anglo-Saxon 'From the pig farm'.

Swithin   Old English 'Strong'.
Swithun

Tabor   Turkish 'A fortified encampment'.

Tadd   Celtic 'Father'. Also diminutive of Thaddeus and Theodore.
Tad

Taggart   Gaelic 'Son of the prelate'.

Talbot   French 'The looter'. One who lived by his spoils and pillages.
Talbert

Talfryn   Welsh 'Brow of the hill'.

Tama   Native American 'Thunderbolt'.

Tamar   Hebrew 'Palm tree'.

Tangwyn   Welsh 'Blessed peace'.

Tanner   Anglo-Saxon 'Leather worker'.
Tann

Tari   Arabic 'Conqueror'.

Tarrant   Old Welsh 'Thunder'.

Tate Anglo-Saxon 'Cheerful'.
Tait, Teyte

Tavis Celtic 'Son of David'. Also derivative (Scottish) of Thomas.
Tavish, Tevis

Taylor Anglo-Saxon 'The Tailor'.
Tailor

Teague Celtic 'The poet'.

Telford French 'Iron hewer'.
Taillefer, Telfer, Telfor, Telfour

Templeton Anglo-Saxon 'Town of the temple'.

Tennyson Anglo-Saxon 'Son of Dennis'.
Tenison, Tennison

Terence Latin 'Smooth, polished and tender'.
Terencio, Terrene, Terry

Terrill Teutonic 'Follower of Thor'.
Terell, Terrel, Terrell, Tirell, Tirrel, Tirrell, Tyrell, Tyrrel, Tyrrell

Thaddeus Greek/Hebrew 'Courageous and stout hearted' (Greek) or 'praise to God' (Hebrew).
Tad, Thad, Taddy, Taddeo

Thaine Anglo-Saxon 'Warrior attendant'. A military attendant on a king or ruler.
Thane, Thayne

Thatcher Anglo-Saxon 'A thatcher of roofs'.
Thatch, Thaxter

Theobald Teutonic 'Bold leader of the people'.
Thibaud, Thibaut, Tibbald, Tioboid, Tybalt

Theodore Greek 'Gift of God'.
Dore, Feodor, Feodore, Tadd, Teador, Ted, Teddie, Teddy, Tudor

Theodoric Teutonic 'Ruler of the people'. The elected leader.
Derek, Derk, Derrick, Dirk, Ted, Teddie, Teddy, Tedric, Teodorico, Theodorick

Theon Greek 'Godly man'.

Theron Greek 'The hunter'.

Thomas Hebrew 'The twin'. The devoted brother.
Massey, Tam, Tamas, Tammany, Tammy, Tavis, Thom, Tom, Tomas, Tomaso, Tommy

Thor Scandinavian 'God of thunder'. The ancient Norse god.
Thorin, Tor, Tyrus

Thorndyke Anglo-Saxon 'From the thorny ditch'.

Thorne Anglo-Saxon 'From the thorn tree'.

Thornley Anglo-Saxon 'From the thorny meadow'.
Thorneley, Thornely, Thornly

Thornton Anglo-Saxon 'From the thorny place'.
Thorn

Thorpe Anglo-Saxon 'From the small village'.
Thorp

Thurlow Anglo-Saxon 'From Thor's hill'.

Thurston Anglo-Saxon 'Thor's jewel'.
Thorstein, Thurstan

Tibor Slavonic 'Holy place'.

Tierman Gaelic 'Lord and master'. The overlord or lord of the manor.
Tierney

T
boys

Tiernan Celtic 'Kingly'.

Tilford Anglo-Saxon 'From the good man's farm'.

Timon Greek 'Honour, reward, value'.

Timothy Greek 'Honouring God'.
Tim, Timmie, Timmy, Timoteo, Timotheus, Tiomoid, Tymon

Titus Greek/Latin 'Of the giants' (Greek) or 'saved' (Latin).
Tito

Tobias Hebrew 'God is good'.
Tioboid, Tobe, Tobiah, Tobit, Toby

Toby Popular variation of Tobias.

Todd Latin 'The fox'.

Tolman Old English 'Tax collector'.

Tomkin Anglo-Saxon Diminutive of Thomas.
Tomlin

Toole Celtic 'Lordly'.

Torin Gaelic 'Chief'.
Thorfinn

Torr Anglo-Saxon 'From the tower'.

Townsend Anglo-Saxon 'From the end of the town'.

Tracy Latin 'Bold and courageous'.

Trahern Celtic 'Iron strength'.
Trahearn, Trahearne, Trehearn, Trehearne, Trehern

Travers Latin 'From the crossroads'.
Travis, Travus

Trelawny Cornish 'From the church town'.
Trelawney

Tremayne   Celtic 'From the house in the rock'.
Tremaine

Trent   Latin 'The torrent'.

Trevelyan   Celtic 'From Elian's farm'. An old Cornish name.

Trevor   Gaelic 'Prudent, wise and discreet'. One who can be trusted to keep secrets.
Trefor

Tristan   Celtic 'The noisy one'.
Drostan, Tristen, Tristin

Tristram   Celtic 'The sorrowful one'. Do not confuse with Tristan.

Troy   French 'From the land of the people with curly hair'.

Truman   Anglo-Saxon 'A faithful follower'. A loyal servant.
Trueman, Trumane

Tucker   Anglo-Saxon 'Cloth thickener'. A variation of Fuller.

Tully   Gaelic 'Obedient to the will of God'.

Turner   Latin 'Lathe worker'.

Turpin   Scandinavian 'Thunder-like'. Finnish form of Thor.

Twyford   Anglo-Saxon 'From the twin river'.

Tye   Anglo-Saxon 'From the enclosure'.

Tyler   Anglo-Saxon 'Maker of tiles or bricks'.
Tiler, Ty

Tynam   Gaelic 'Dark, grey'.

Tyrone   Greek 'The sovereign'.

Tyson   Teutonic 'Son of the German'.
Sonny, Ty

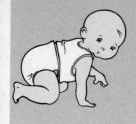

Udell   Anglo-Saxon 'From the yew tree valley'.
Udale, Udall

Ulger   Anglo-Saxon 'Courageous wolf (spearman)'.

Ullock   Anglo-Saxon 'Sport of the wolf'.

Ulmer   Anglo-Saxon 'Famous wolf'.
Ulmar

Ulric   Teutonic 'Ruler of all'.
Alric, Ulrich

Ulysses   Greek 'The angry one, the hater'.
Uillioc, Ulick, Ulises

Unwin   Anglo-Saxon 'The enemy'.

Upton   Anglo-Saxon 'From the hill farm'.

Upwood   Anglo-Saxon 'From the hill forest'.

Urban   Latin 'From the city'. A townsman.
Urbano

Uri   Hebrew 'Light'.

Uriah   Hebrew 'The Lord is my light' or 'the Lord's light'.
Urias, Uriel

boys

Vail	Anglo-Saxon 'From the valley'. *Vale, Valle*
Val	Teutonic 'Mighty power'. Also diminutive for any name beginning with 'Val'.
Valdemar	Teutonic 'Famous ruler'. *Valdimar, Waldemar*
Valentine	Latin 'Healthy, strong and valorous'. *Vailintin, Valente, Valentin, Valentino, Valiant*
Valerian	Latin 'Strong and powerful' or 'belonging to Valentine'.
Vance	Anglo-Saxon 'From the grain barn'.
Varden	Anglo-Saxon 'From a green hill'. *Vardon, Verden, Verdon*
Varian	Latin 'Changeable'.
Vaughan	Celtic 'The small one'. *Vaughn, Vawn*

Venn   Old English 'Handsome'.

Vernon   Latin 'Growing, flourishing'. Like trees in spring.
Vern, Verne, Verner

Victor   Latin 'The conqueror'.
Vic, Vick, Victoir, Vince, Vincent, Vittorio

Vincent   Latin 'Conquering'.

Virgil   Latin 'Staff bearer' or 'strong and flourishing'.
Vergil, Virge, Virgie, Virgy

Vito   Latin 'Alive, vital'.

Vivien   Latin 'Lively one'.
Ninian, Vivian

Vladimir   Slavic 'Royally famous'. A renowned monarch.
Vadim

Wade Anglo-Saxon 'Mover, wanderer'.

Wadley Anglo-Saxon 'From the wanderer's meadow'.

Wadsworth Anglo-Saxon 'From the wanderer's estate'.

Wagner Teutonic 'A waggoner'.

Wainwright Anglo-Saxon 'Waggon maker'.

Waite Anglo-Saxon 'A guard, a watchman'.

Wakefield Anglo-Saxon 'From the west field'.
Wake

Wakeley Anglo-Saxon 'From the wet meadow'.

Wakeman Anglo-Saxon 'Watchman'.

Walcott Anglo-Saxon 'Cottage dweller'.

Walden Anglo-Saxon 'One who lives in the valley in the woods'.

Waldo Teutonic 'The ruler'.

Walker Anglo-Saxon 'The walker'.

Wallace Anglo-Saxon 'The Welshman' or 'the stranger'.
Wallache, Wallie, Wallis, Wally, Walsh, Welch, Welsh

Walter Teutonic 'Mighty warrior'.
Wally, Walt, Walters, Walther, Wat

Walton Anglo-Saxon 'From the forest town'.

Walworth Anglo-Saxon 'From the stranger's farm'.

Ward Anglo-Saxon 'Watchman, guardian'.

Wardell Anglo-Saxon 'From the hill watch'.

Warden Anglo-Saxon 'The guardian'.

Ware Anglo-Saxon 'Prudent one'. A very astute person.

Warley Anglo-Saxon 'From the meadow by the weir'.

Warner Teutonic 'Protecting army'.
Verner, Werner

Warren Teutonic 'The gamekeeper'. One who looked after the game preserves.
Waring

Warwick Anglo-Saxon 'Strong fortress'.
Warrick

Washington Anglo-Saxon 'From the keen-eyed one's farm'.

Watford Anglo-Saxon 'From the hurdle by the ford'.

Watkins Anglo-Saxon 'Son of Walter'.
Watson

Waverley Anglo-Saxon 'The meadow by the aspen trees'.
Waverly

Wayland	Anglo-Saxon	'From the pathway near the highway'.
		Weylin
Wayne	Teutonic	'Waggon maker'.
		Wain, Waine
Webb	Anglo-Saxon	'A weaver'.
		Webber, Weber, Webster
Webster	Old English	'Weaver'.
Welby	Anglo-Saxon	'From the farm by the spring'.
Weldon	Anglo-Saxon	'From the well on the hill'.
Wellington	Anglo-Saxon	'From the rich man's farm'.
Wells	Anglo-Saxon	'From the spring'.
Wendell	Teutonic	'The wanderer'.
		Wendall
Wentworth	Anglo-Saxon	'Estate belonging to the white-haired one'.
Wesley	Anglo-Saxon	'From the west meadow'.
		Wesleigh, Westleigh
Westbrook	Anglo-Saxon	'From the west brook'.
Westby	Anglo-Saxon	'From the homestead in the west'.
Westcott	Anglo-Saxon	'From the west cottage'.
Weston	Anglo-Saxon	'From the west farm'.
Wetherell	Anglo-Saxon	'From the sheep hill'.
		Wetherall, Wetherill
Wetherley	Anglo-Saxon	'From the sheep meadow'.
		Wetherly

Wheatley Anglo-Saxon 'From the wheat meadow'.

Whitby Anglo-Saxon 'From the white farmstead'.

Whitelaw Anglo-Saxon 'From the white hill'.

Whitford Anglo-Saxon 'From the white ford'.

Whitlock Anglo-Saxon 'White-haired one'.

Whitman Anglo-Saxon 'White-haired man'.

Whitmore Anglo-Saxon 'From the white moor'.

Whitney Anglo-Saxon 'From the white island'.
Whitny, Witney, Witny

Whittaker Anglo-Saxon 'One who dwells in the white field'.
Whitaker

Wickham Anglo-Saxon 'From the enclosed field by the village'.
Wykeham

Wickley Anglo-Saxon 'From the village meadow'.

Wilbur Teutonic 'Resolute and brilliant'. A determined and clever person.
Wilbert

Wilfred Teutonic 'Firm peace maker'. Peace, but not at any price.
Fred, Freddie, Freddy, Wilfrid

Willard Anglo-Saxon 'Resolute and brave'.

William Teutonic 'Determined protector'. The strong guardian.
Bill, Billie, Billy, Guillym, Gwylim, Liam, Uilleam, Uilliam, Wiley, Wilhelm, Wilkes, Wilkie, Will, Willet, Williamson, Willie, Willis, Willy, Wilson

Willoughby Anglo-Saxon 'From the farmstead by the willows'.

Wilmer	Teutonic	'Resolute and famous'. One renowned for his firmness.
Wilmot	Teutonic	'Resolute mind'. One who knows his own mind.
Wilson	Anglo-Saxon	'Son of William'.
Windsor	Anglo-Saxon	'The boundary bank'.
Winfred	Anglo-Saxon	'Peaceful friend'.
Winslow	Anglo-Saxon	'From a friend's hill'.
Winston	Anglo-Saxon	'From a friend's estate'.
Winter	Anglo-Saxon	'Born during winter months'.
Winthrop	Teutonic	'From a friendly village'.
Winton	Anglo-Saxon	'From a friend's farm'.
Winward	Anglo-Saxon	'From the friendly forest'. *Winwald*
Wolfe	Teutonic	'A wolf'. A man of courage.
Wolfgang	Teutonic	'The advancing wolf'. A warrior in the vanguard of the army.
Woodruff	Anglo-Saxon	'Forest bailiff'.
Woodward	Anglo-Saxon	'Forest guardian'.
Worcester	Anglo-Saxon	'Camp in the forest of the alder trees'. *Wooster*
Wordsworth	Anglo-Saxon	'From the farm of the wolf'.
Wray	Scandinavian	'One who lives in the house on the corner'.
Wright	Anglo-Saxon	'Craftsman in woodwork, a carpenter'.
Wybert	Old English	'Battle famous'.

Wycliff Anglo-Saxon 'From the white cliff'.

Wyman Anglo-Saxon 'The warrior'.

Wyndham Anglo-Saxon 'From the village with the winding path'.
Windham

Wynn Celtic 'The fair one'.

boys

Xanthus	Latin 'Golden haired'.
Xavier	Arabic/Spanish 'Bright'. *Javier*
Xenophon	Greek 'Strong sounding'.
Xenos	Greek 'The stranger'.
Xerxes	Persian 'The king'.
Xylon	Greek 'From the forest'.

boys

Yale Teutonic/Anglo-Saxon 'The one who pays, the vanquished'.

Yancy Native American 'The Englishman'. Name given to settlers in New England and subsequently became Yankee.
Yance

Yardley Old English 'From the enclosed meadow'.

Yarin Hebrew 'Understand'.

Yasir Arabic 'Easy, soft'.

Yates Anglo-Saxon 'One who lives at the gates'.

Yehudi Hebrew 'Praise to the Lord'.

Yeoman Anglo-Saxon 'The tenant farmer'.

Yestin Welsh 'Just'.

Ynyr Welsh 'Honour'.

York Anglo-Saxon/Celtic/Latin 'Sacred yew tree'.
Yorick, Yorke

Yul Mongolian 'Beyond the horizon'.

Yules Anglo-Saxon 'Born at Christmas'.
Yule

Yuma Native American 'Son of a chief'.

Yvon Teutonic "the archer".

Ywain Celtic 'Young warrior'.

Z

Zachaeus Aramaic 'Pure'.

Zacharias Hebrew 'The Lord has remembered'.
Zach, Zachariah, Zachary, Zack

Zadok Hebrew 'The righteous one'.
Zaloc

Zahid Sanskrit/Arabic 'Intelligent and pious'.

Zahir Arabic 'Splendid'.

Zebediah Hebrew 'Gift of the Lord'.
Zebedee

Zebulon Hebrew 'The dwelling place'.
Lonny, Zeb, Zebulen

Zechariah Hebrew 'The Lord is renowned'.

Zedekiah Hebrew 'The Lord's justice'.

Zeeman Dutch 'The sailor'.

Zelig Teutonic 'Blessed one'.

Zelotes Greek 'The zealous one'.

Zenas Greek 'Living being'.

Zeno Greek 'Stranger'.

Zeus Greek 'Father of the gods'.

Zia Sanskrit 'Enlightened'.

Zimraan Arabic 'Celebrated'.

Zuriel Hebrew 'The Lord is my rock and foundation'.